MAX AXIOM
AND THE SOCIETY OF SUPER SCIENTISTS

SUPERBUGS AND PANDEMICS

BY **EMILY SOHN**
ILLUSTRATED BY **EDUARDO GARCIA**

CAPSTONE PRESS
a capstone imprint

Published by Capstone Press, an imprint of Capstone.
1710 Roe Crest Drive
North Mankato, Minnesota 56003
capstonepub.com

Library of Congress Cataloging-in-Publication Data
Names: Sohn, Emily, author.
Title: Superbugs and pandemics : a max axiom super scientist adventure / Emily Sohn.
Description: North Mankato : Capstone Press, 2022. | Series: Max axiom and the society of super scientists | Includes bibliographical references and index. | Audience: Ages 8-11 | Audience: Grades 4-6
Summary: "A new disease has reared its ugly head. People are getting very sick with high fevers and an itchy rash. Even worse, it seems to be spreading quickly to several major cities around the world. What is this new disease, and why is it spreading so fast? It's up to Max Axiom and the Society of Super Scientists to find out! In this nonfiction graphic novel, young readers can follow the team as they go on an exciting, fact-filled adventure to learn how diseases work, why pandemics and superbugs are so dangerous, and things they can do to help stop the spread of deadly disease"-- Provided by publisher.
Identifiers: LCCN 2021033322 (print) | LCCN 2021033323 (ebook) | ISBN 9781663959201 (hardcover) | ISBN 9781666322767 (paperback) | ISBN 9781666322774 (pdf) | ISBN 9781666322798 (kindle edition)
Subjects: LCSH: Drug resistance in microorganisms--Juvenile literature. | Epidemics--Juvenile literature.
Classification: LCC QR177 .S63 2022 (print) | LCC QR177 (ebook) | DDC 616.9/041--dc23
LC record available at https://lccn.loc.gov/2021033322
LC ebook record available at https://lccn.loc.gov/2021033323

Editorial Credits
Editor: Aaron Sautter; Designer: Brann Garvey; Media Researcher: Morgan Walters; Production Specialist: Laura Manthe

All internet sites appearing in back matter were available and accurate when this book was sent to press.

TABLE OF CONTENTS

THE SOCIETY OF SUPER SCIENTISTS

MAX AXIOM

After years of study, Max Axiom, the world's first Super Scientist, knew the mysteries of the universe were too vast for one person alone to uncover. So Max created the Society of Super Scientists! Using their superpowers and super-smarts, this talented group investigates today's most urgent scientific and environmental issues and learns about actions everyone can take to solve them.

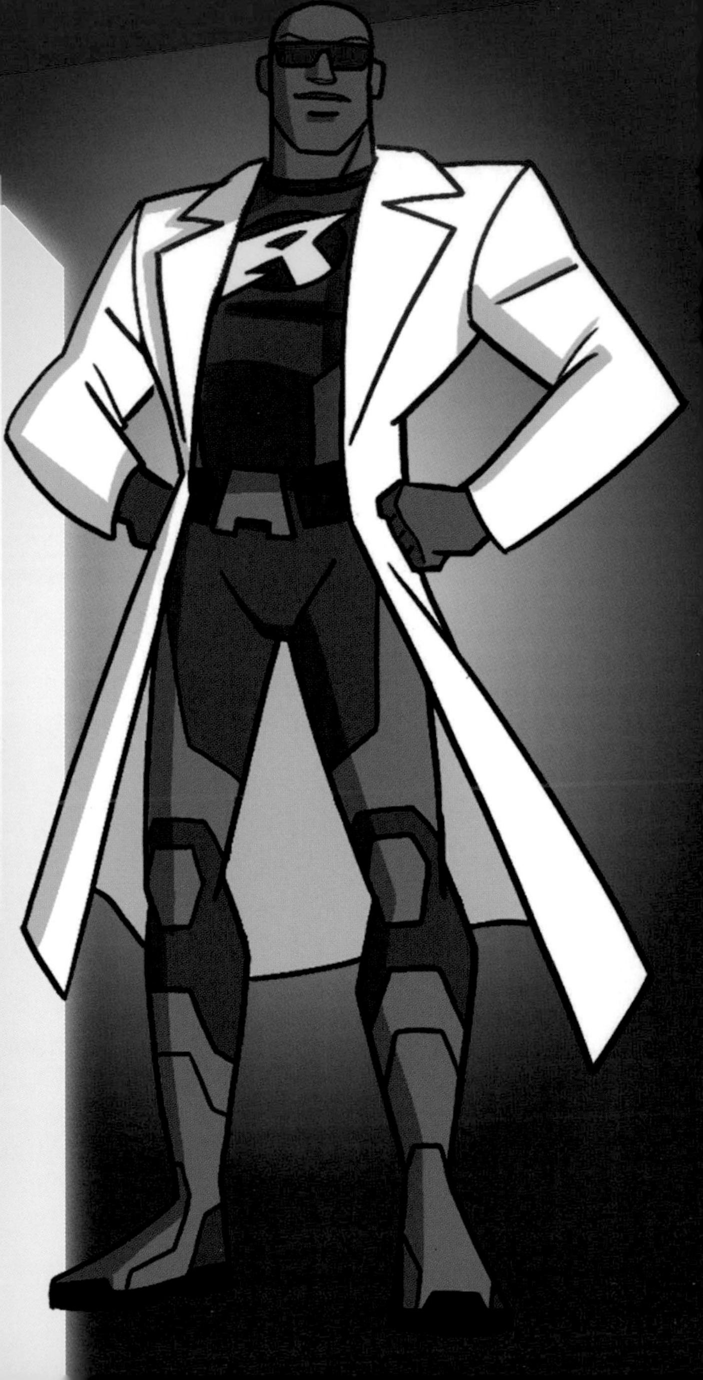

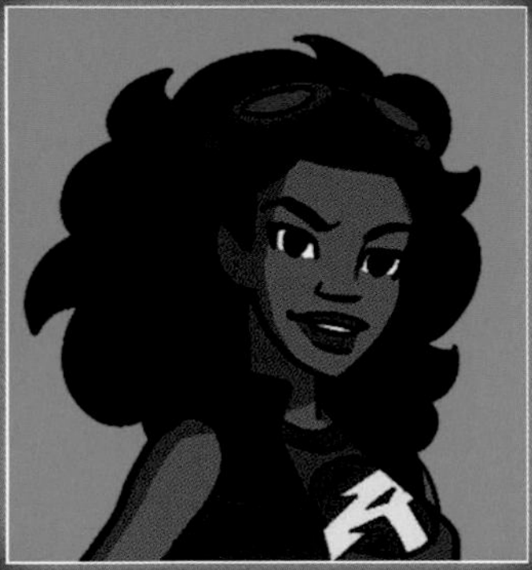

LIZZY AXIOM

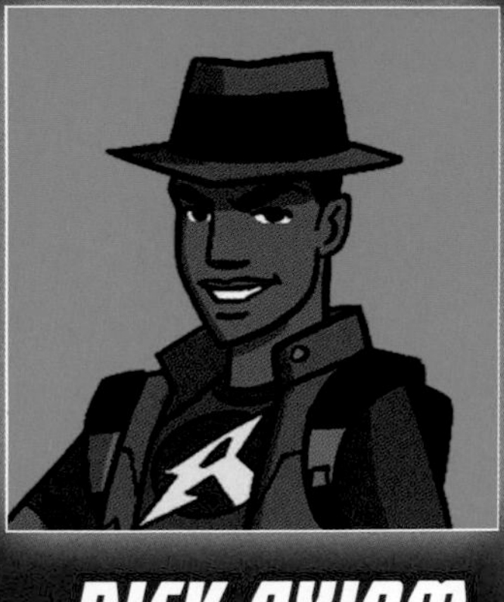

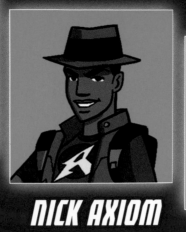

NICK AXIOM

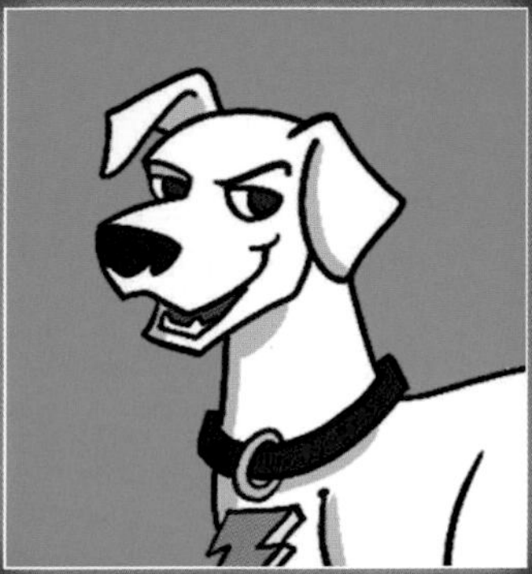

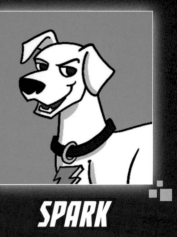

SPARK

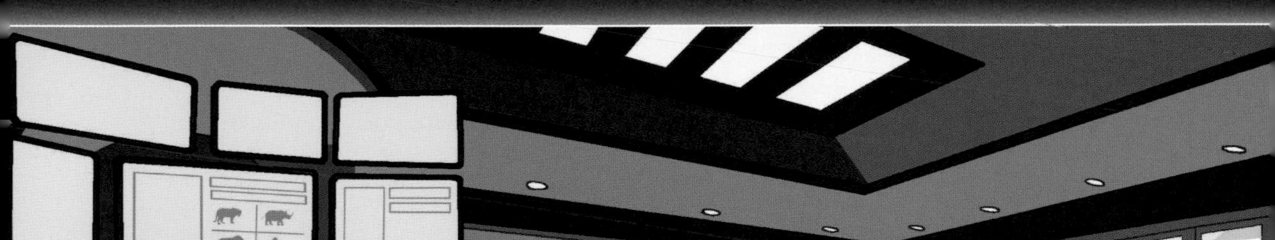

LAB

THE DISCOVERY LAB

Home of the Society of Super Scientists, this state-of-the-art lab houses advanced tools for cutting-edge research and radical scientific innovation. More importantly, it is a space for Super Scientists to collaborate and share knowledge as they work together to tackle any challenge.

SECTION 1: A NEW DISEASE

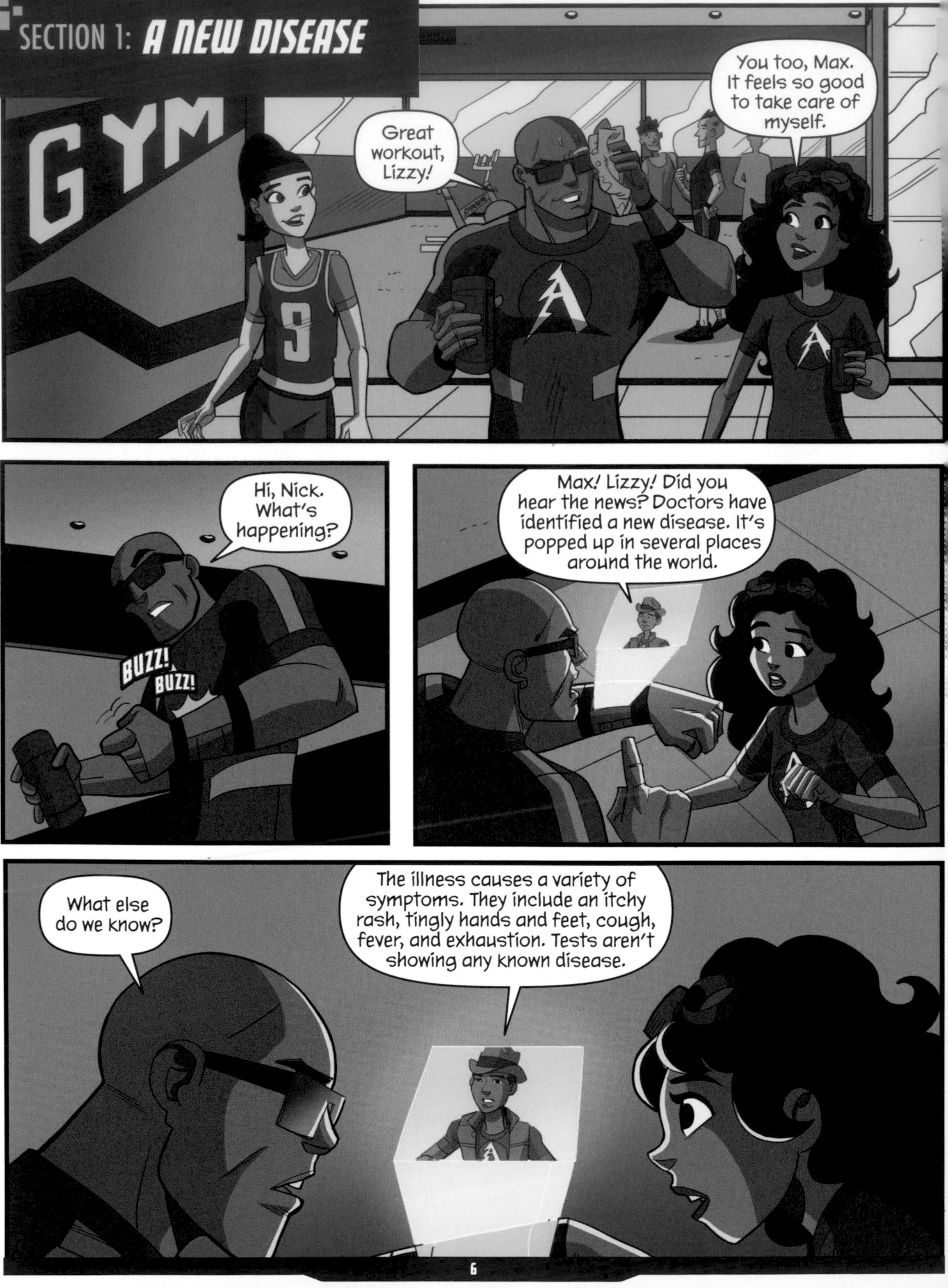

GYM
Great workout, Lizzy!
You too, Max. It feels so good to take care of myself.
Hi, Nick. What's happening?
BUZZ!
BUZZ!
Max! Lizzy! Did you hear the news? Doctors have identified a new disease. It's popped up in several places around the world.
What else do we know?
The illness causes a variety of symptoms. They include an itchy rash, tingly hands and feet, cough, fever, and exhaustion. Tests aren't showing any known disease.

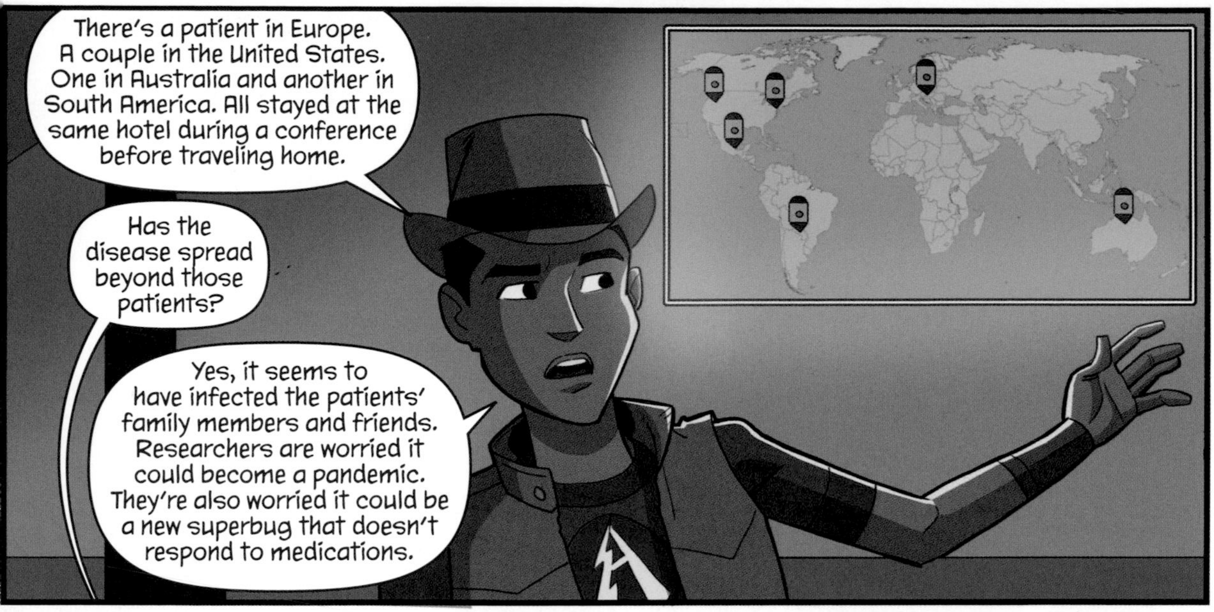
There's a patient in Europe. A couple in the United States. One in Australia and another in South America. All stayed at the same hotel during a conference before traveling home.
Has the disease spread beyond those patients?
Yes, it seems to have infected the patients' family members and friends. Researchers are worried it could become a pandemic. They're also worried it could be a new superbug that doesn't respond to medications.

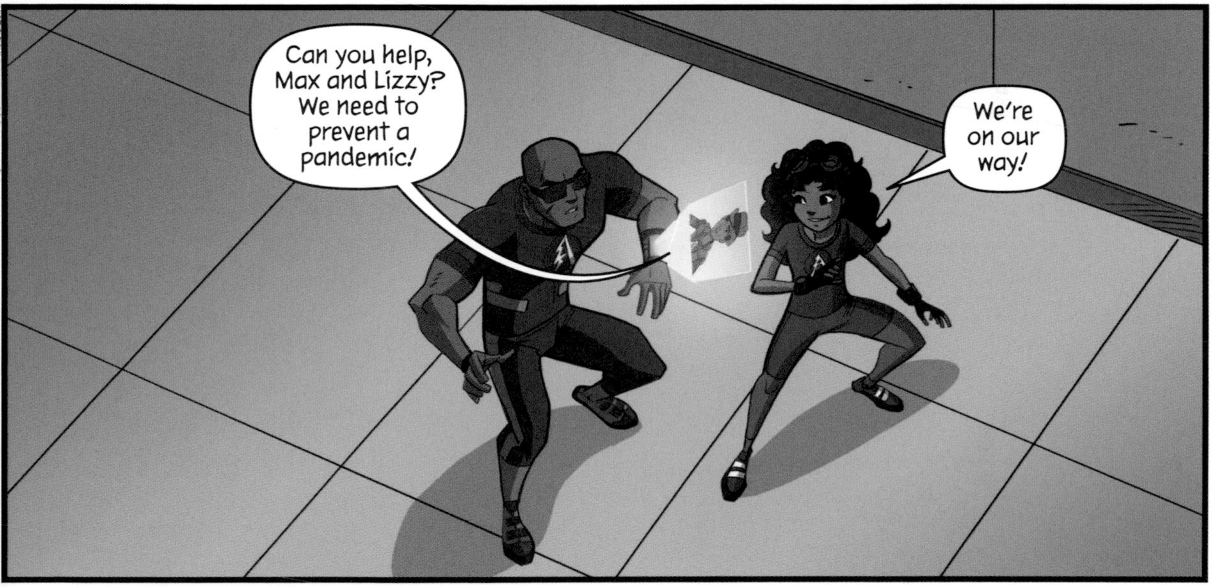
Can you help, Max and Lizzy? We need to prevent a pandemic!
We're on our way!

DISEASE DEFINITIONS

Scientists use a variety of words to describe the spread of diseases.

Epidemic: An increase in the number of cases of a disease above the normal rate in a population.

Outbreak: An epidemic in a limited geographic area.

Pandemic: An epidemic that has spread into several countries. It usually affects large numbers of people.

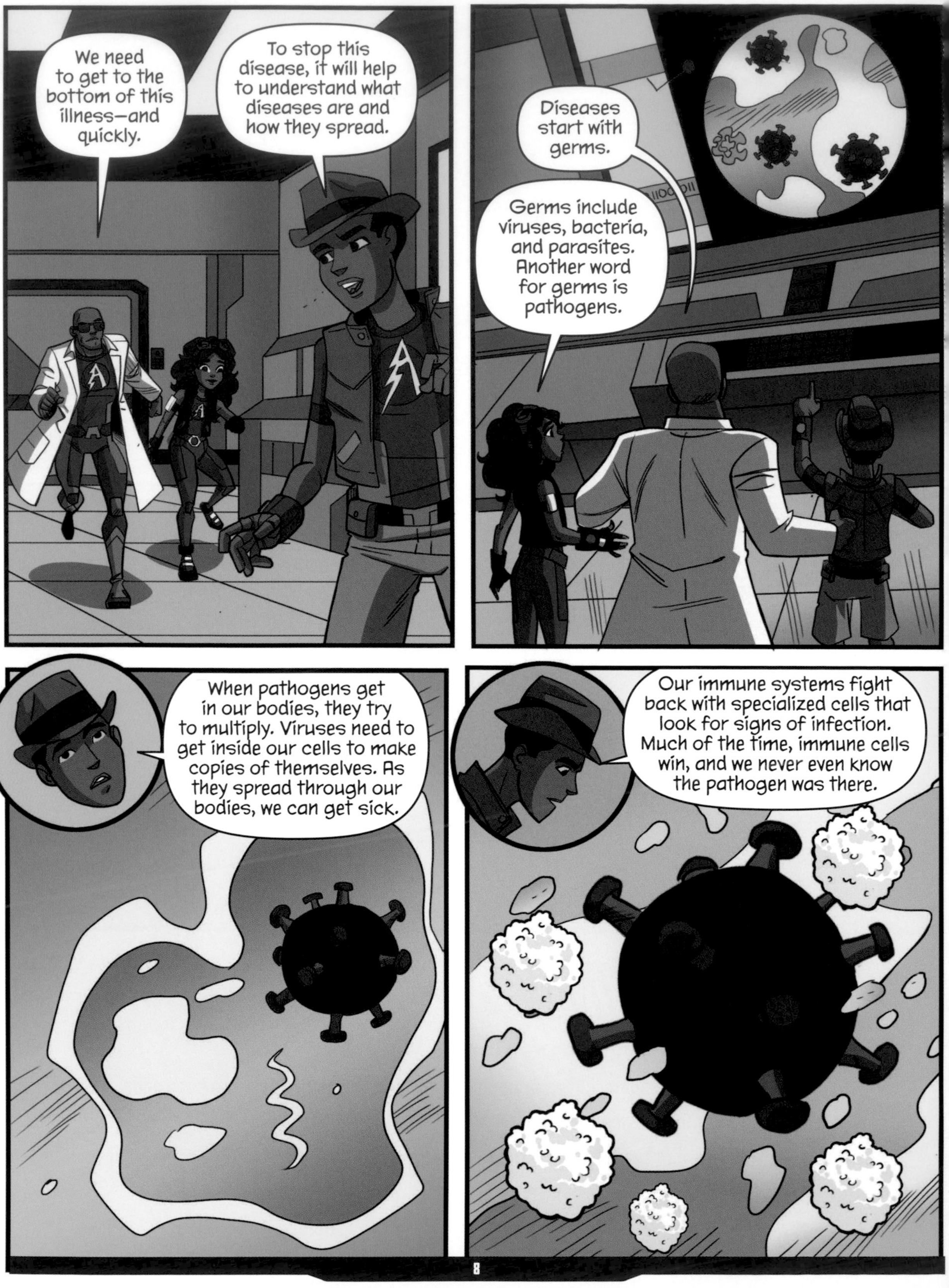

We need to get to the bottom of this illness—and quickly.
To stop this disease, it will help to understand what diseases are and how they spread.
Diseases start with germs.
Germs include viruses, bacteria, and parasites. Another word for germs is pathogens.
When pathogens get in our bodies, they try to multiply. Viruses need to get inside our cells to make copies of themselves. As they spread through our bodies, we can get sick.
Our immune systems fight back with specialized cells that look for signs of infection. Much of the time, immune cells win, and we never even know the pathogen was there.

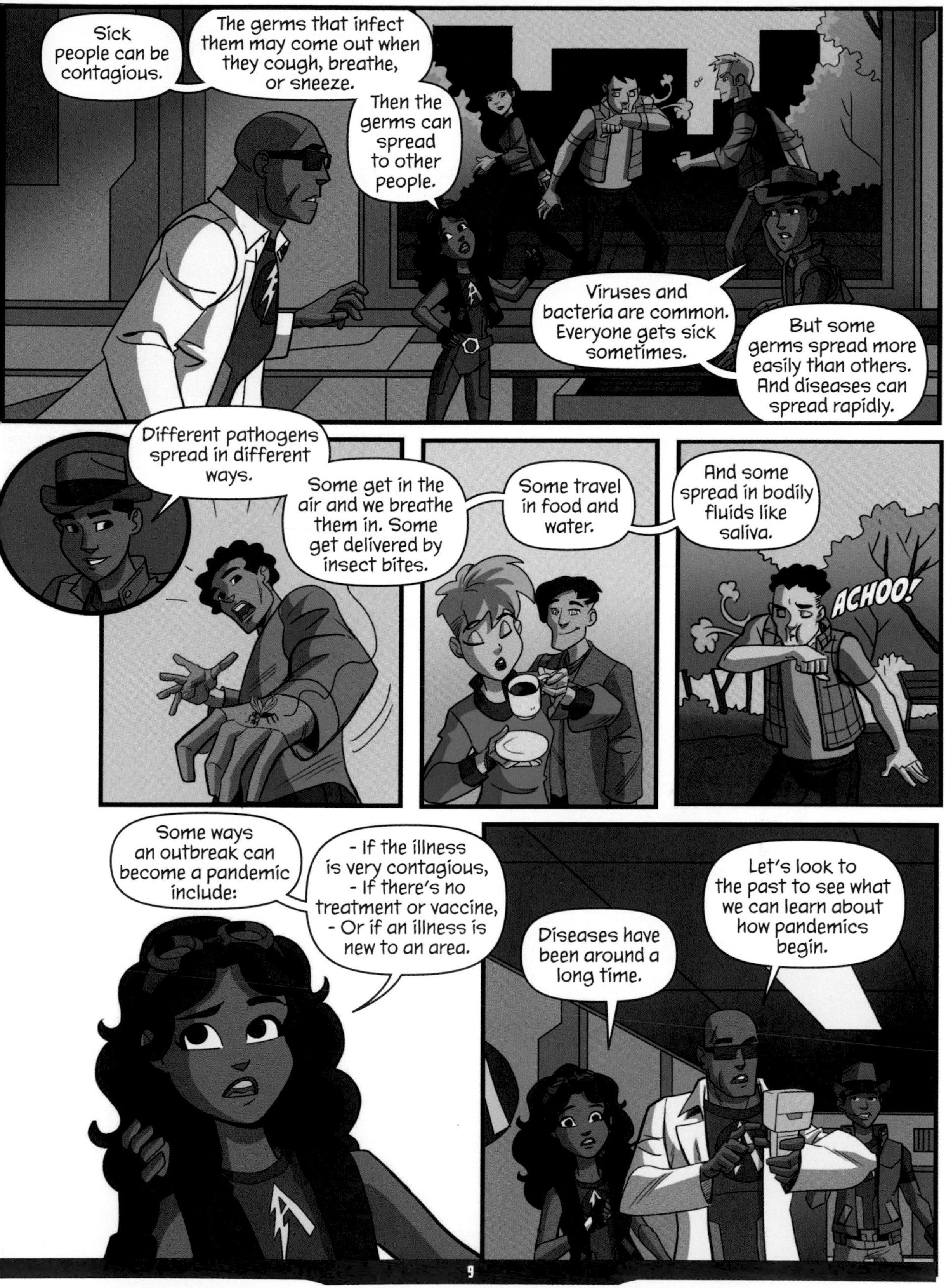
Sick people can be contagious.
The germs that infect them may come out when they cough, breathe, or sneeze.
Then the germs can spread to other people.
Viruses and bacteria are common. Everyone gets sick sometimes.
But some germs spread more easily than others. And diseases can spread rapidly.
Different pathogens spread in different ways.
Some get in the air and we breathe them in. Some get delivered by insect bites.
Some travel in food and water.
And some spread in bodily fluids like saliva.
ACHOO!
Some ways an outbreak can become a pandemic include:
- If the illness is very contagious,
- If there's no treatment or vaccine,
- Or if an illness is new to an area.
Diseases have been around a long time.
Let's look to the past to see what we can learn about how pandemics begin.

SECTION 2: DISEASES THROUGH TIME

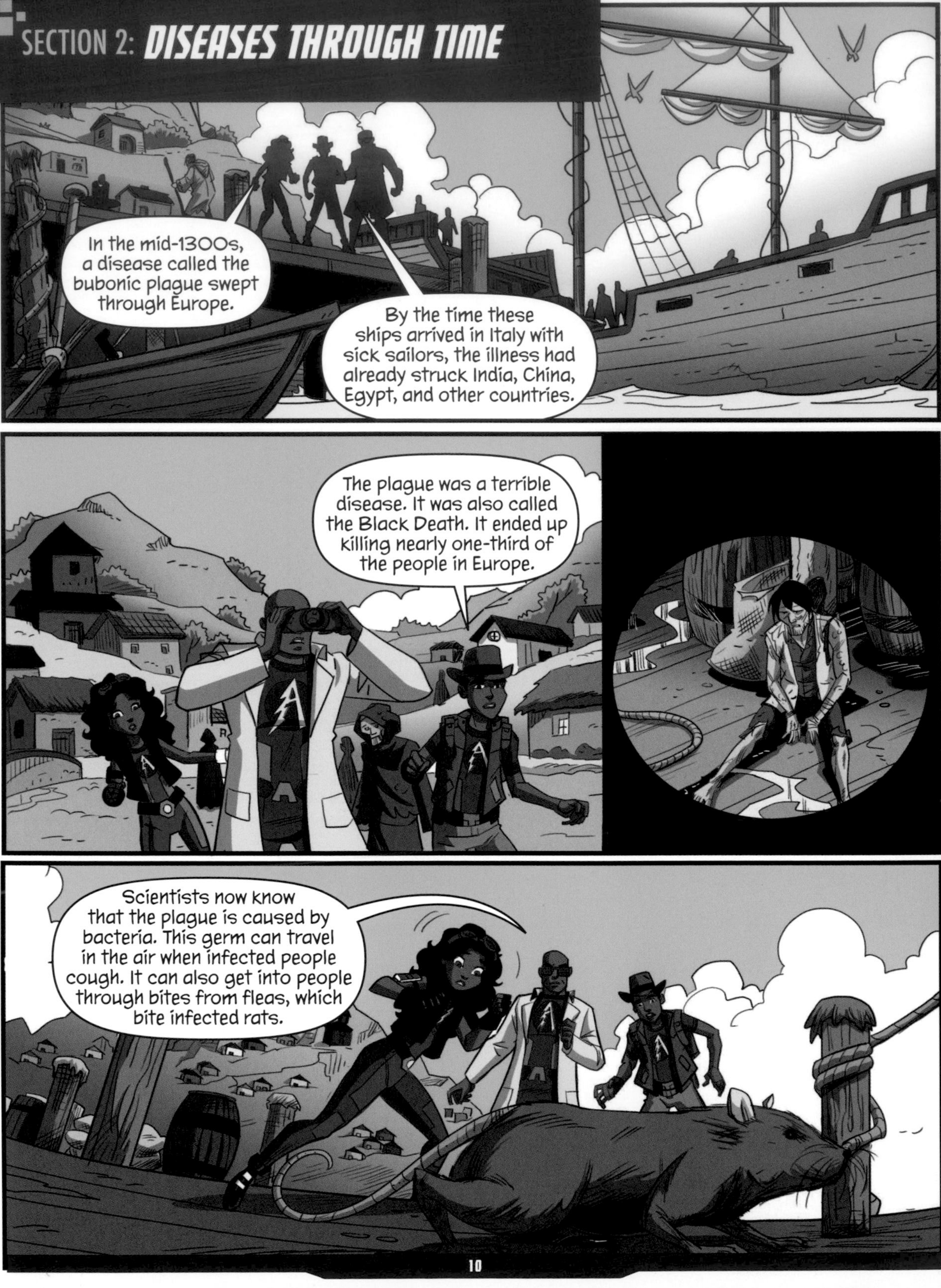
In the mid-1300s, a disease called the bubonic plague swept through Europe.
By the time these ships arrived in Italy with sick sailors, the illness had already struck India, China, Egypt, and other countries.
The plague was a terrible disease. It was also called the Black Death. It ended up killing nearly one-third of the people in Europe.
Scientists now know that the plague is caused by bacteria. This germ can travel in the air when infected people cough. It can also get into people through bites from fleas, which bite infected rats.

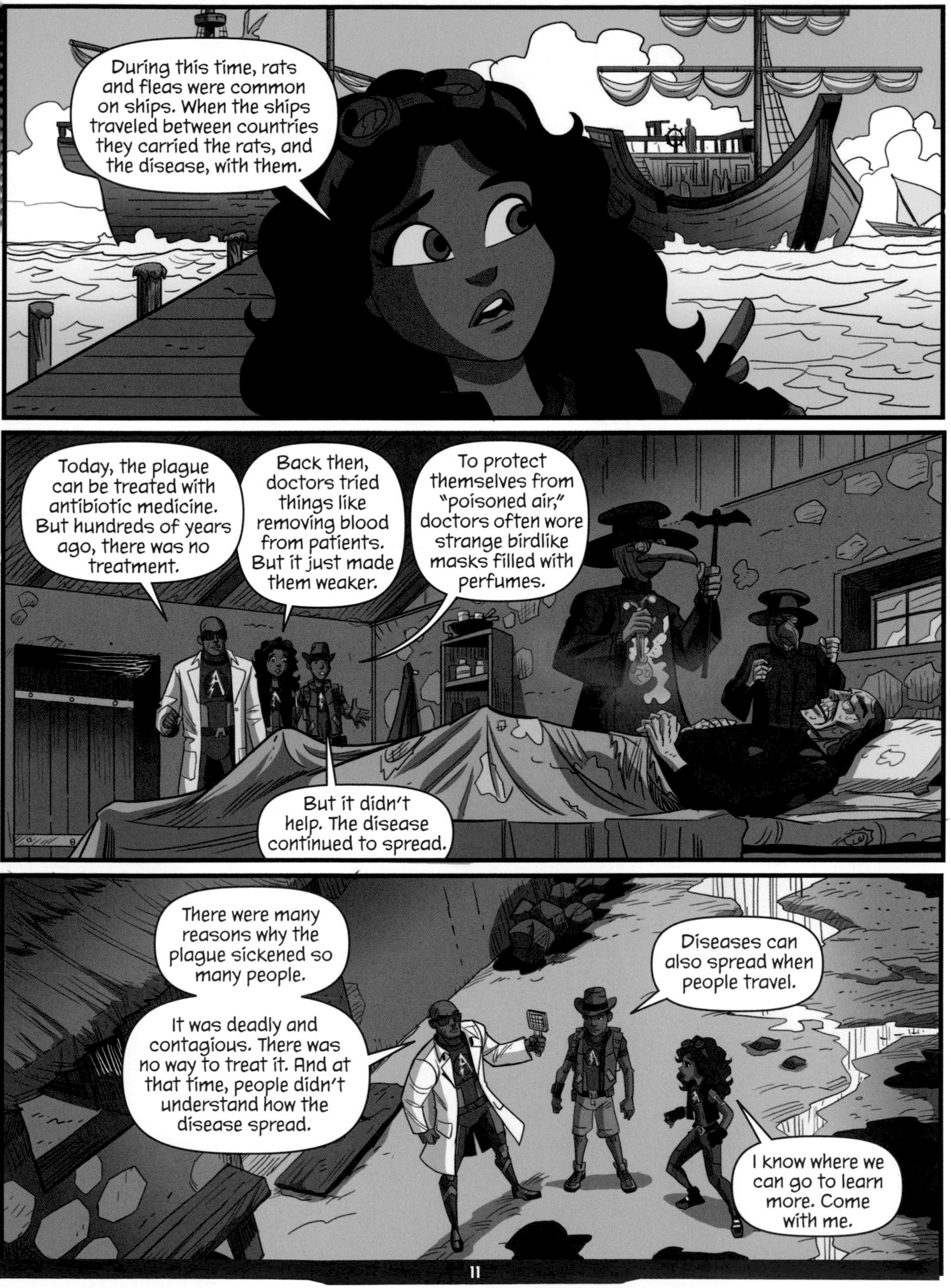
During this time, rats and fleas were common on ships. When the ships traveled between countries they carried the rats, and the disease, with them.
Today, the plague can be treated with antibiotic medicine. But hundreds of years ago, there was no treatment.
Back then, doctors tried things like removing blood from patients. But it just made them weaker.
To protect themselves from "poisoned air," doctors often wore strange birdlike masks filled with perfumes.
But it didn't help. The disease continued to spread.
There were many reasons why the plague sickened so many people.
It was deadly and contagious. There was no way to treat it. And at that time, people didn't understand how the disease spread.
Diseases can also spread when people travel.
I know where we can go to learn more. Come with me.

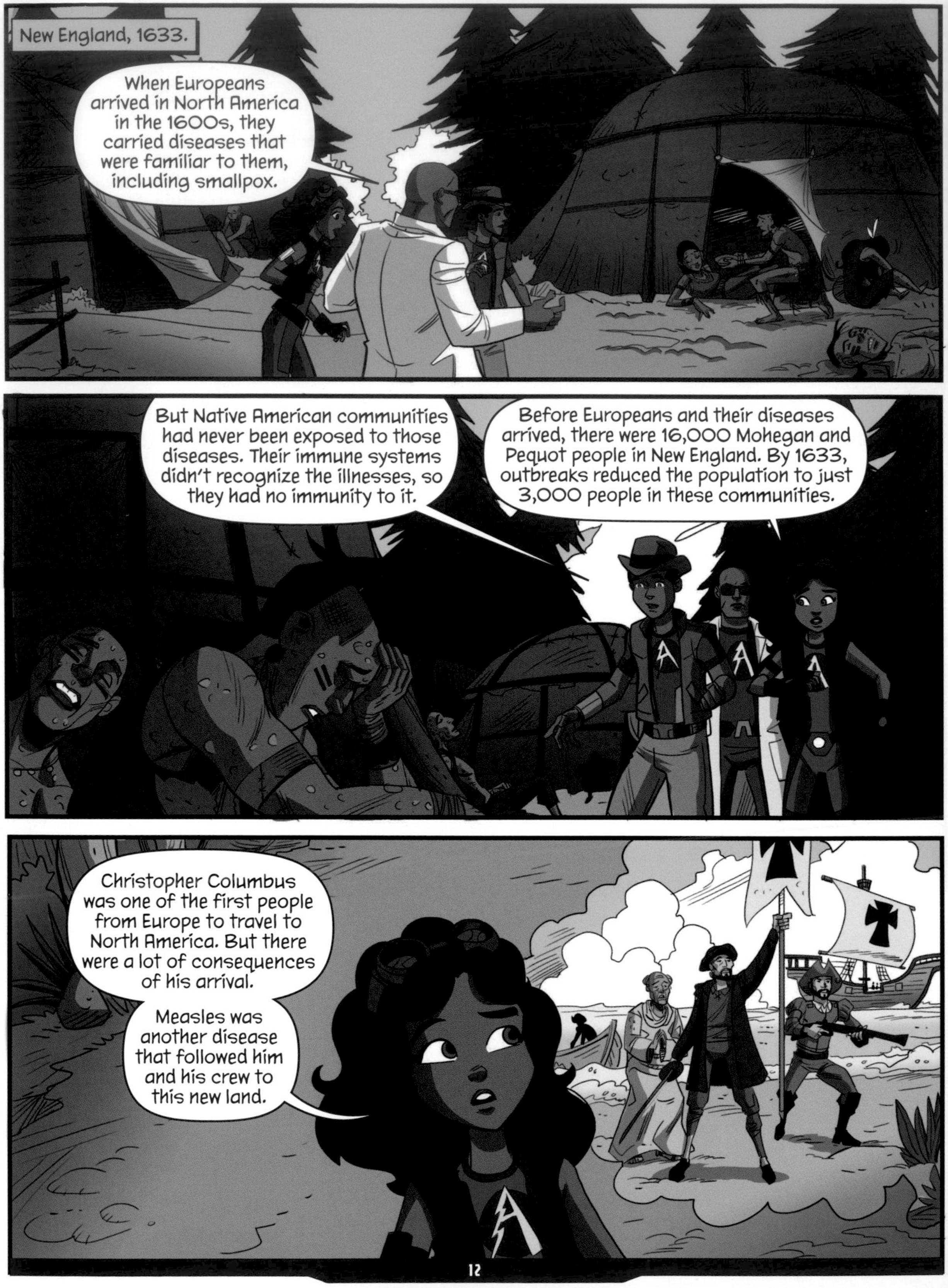
New England, 1633.
When Europeans arrived in North America in the 1600s, they carried diseases that were familiar to them, including smallpox.
But Native American communities had never been exposed to those diseases. Their immune systems didn't recognize the illnesses, so they had no immunity to it.
Before Europeans and their diseases arrived, there were 16,000 Mohegan and Pequot people in New England. By 1633, outbreaks reduced the population to just 3,000 people in these communities.
Christopher Columbus was one of the first people from Europe to travel to North America. But there were a lot of consequences of his arrival.
Measles was another disease that followed him and his crew to this new land.

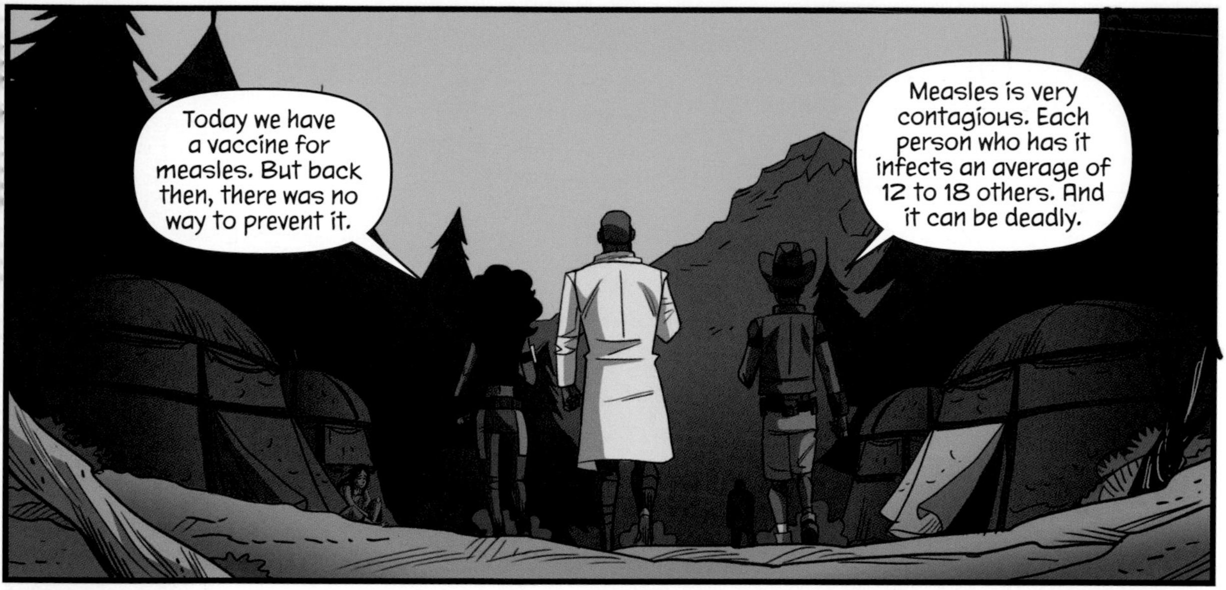
Today we have a vaccine for measles. But back then, there was no way to prevent it.
Measles is very contagious. Each person who has it infects an average of 12 to 18 others. And it can be deadly.

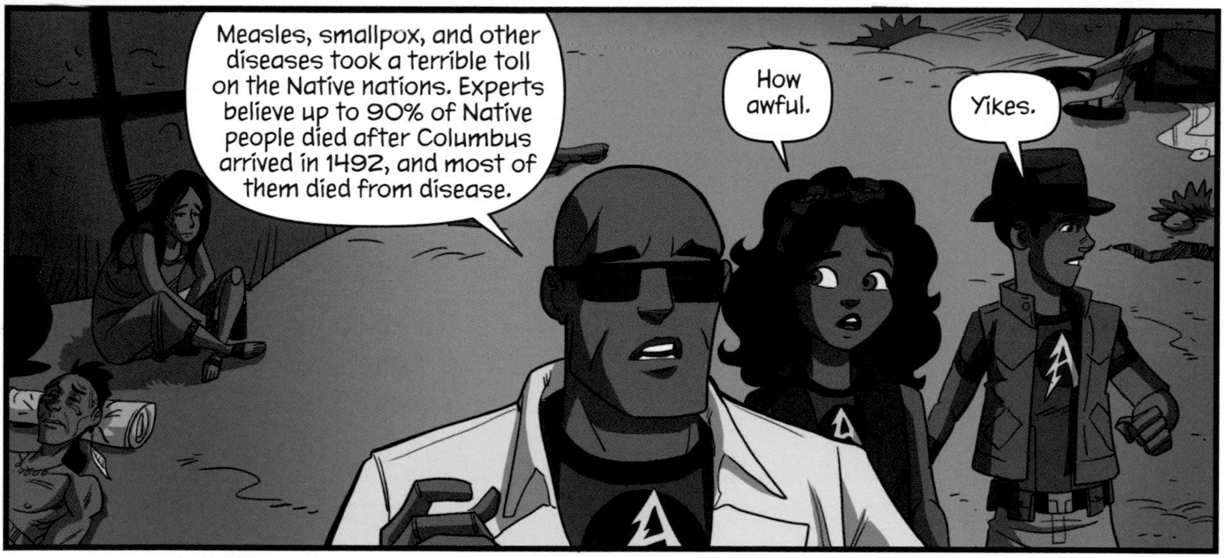
Measles, smallpox, and other diseases took a terrible toll on the Native nations. Experts believe up to 90% of Native people died after Columbus arrived in 1492, and most of them died from disease.
How awful.
Yikes.

CONTAGIOUS STATS

Some diseases spread more easily than others. R0 is the term scientists use to describe how contagious a disease is. The R0 number shows the average number of other people that may get a disease from an infected person.

1918 flu: R0 = 1-2
Ebola virus: R0 = 1.5-2.5
Measles: R0 = 12-18
SARS: R0 = 1-2.75
Smallpox: R0 = 5-7
COVID-19: R0 = 2-3 (estimated)

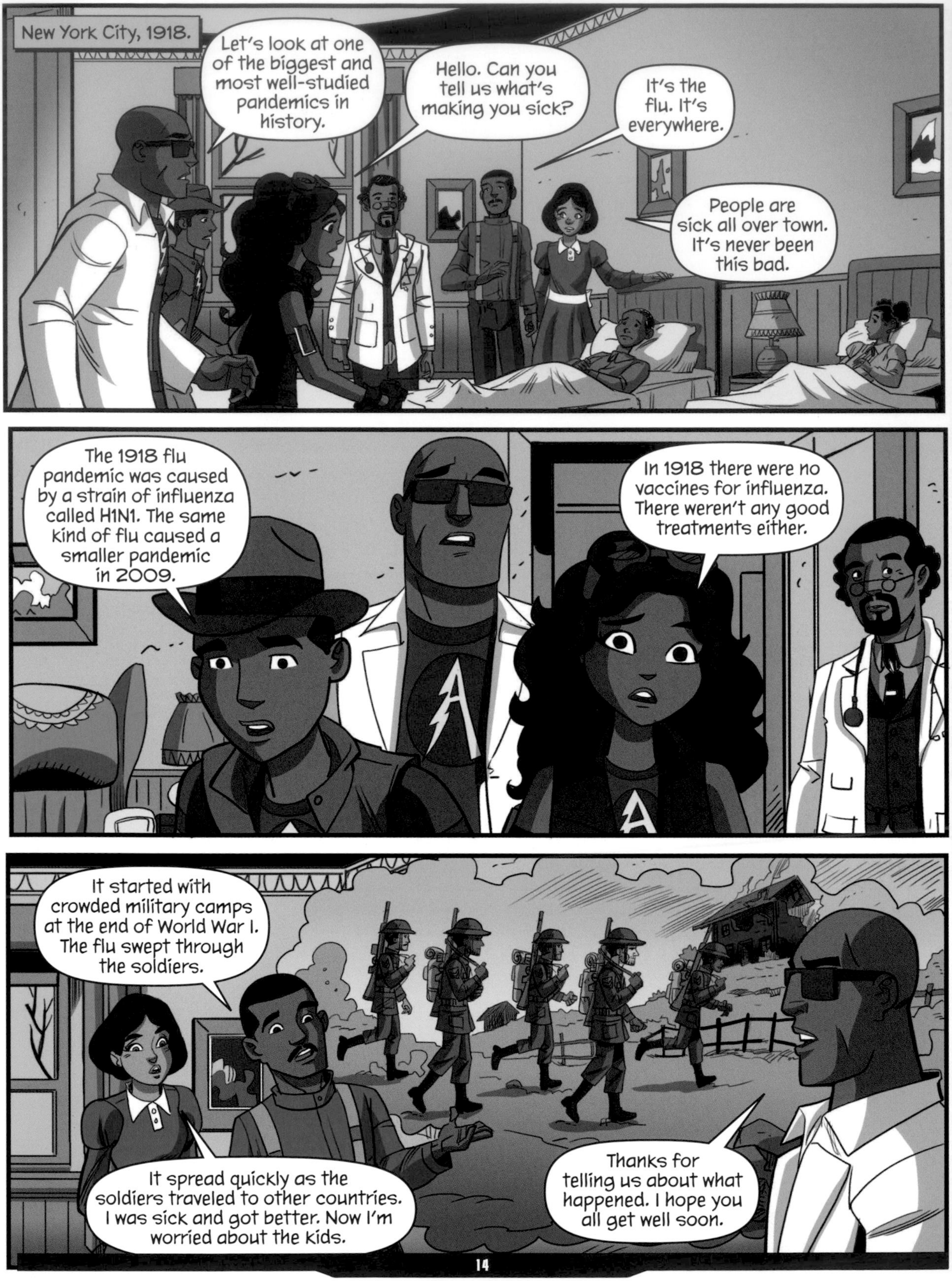
New York City, 1918.
Let's look at one of the biggest and most well-studied pandemics in history.
Hello. Can you tell us what's making you sick?
It's the flu. It's everywhere.
People are sick all over town. It's never been this bad.
The 1918 flu pandemic was caused by a strain of influenza called H1N1. The same kind of flu caused a smaller pandemic in 2009.
In 1918 there were no vaccines for influenza. There weren't any good treatments either.
It started with crowded military camps at the end of World War I. The flu swept through the soldiers.
It spread quickly as the soldiers traveled to other countries. I was sick and got better. Now I'm worried about the kids.
Thanks for telling us about what happened. I hope you all get well soon.

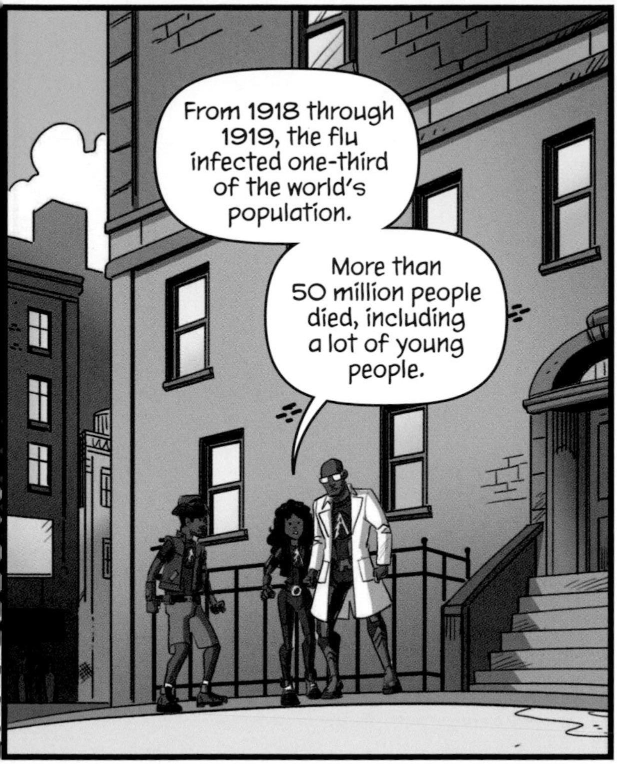
From 1918 through 1919, the flu infected one-third of the world's population.
More than 50 million people died, including a lot of young people.

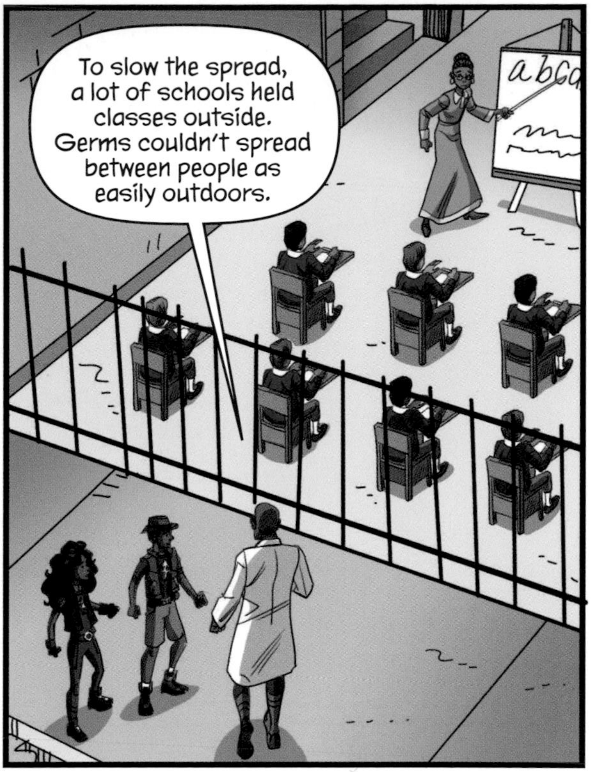
To slow the spread, a lot of schools held classes outside. Germs couldn't spread between people as easily outdoors.

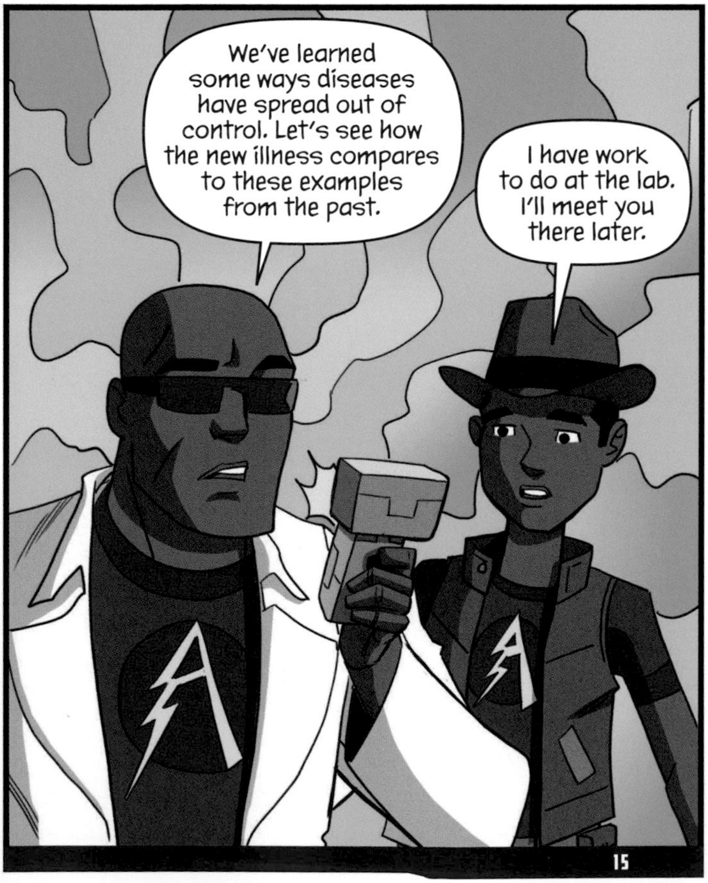
We've learned some ways diseases have spread out of control. Let's see how the new illness compares to these examples from the past.
I have work to do at the lab. I'll meet you there later.

THE FLU

Influenza is the name of the virus that causes the flu. Many people get a flu shot in the fall or winter. Influenza comes in many forms, called strains. Often, the virus mutates, or changes into a new strain. Each year, scientists try to predict which strains will spread. They create a new vaccine each year that helps the body fight off those strains.

SECTION 3: DISEASE INVESTIGATION

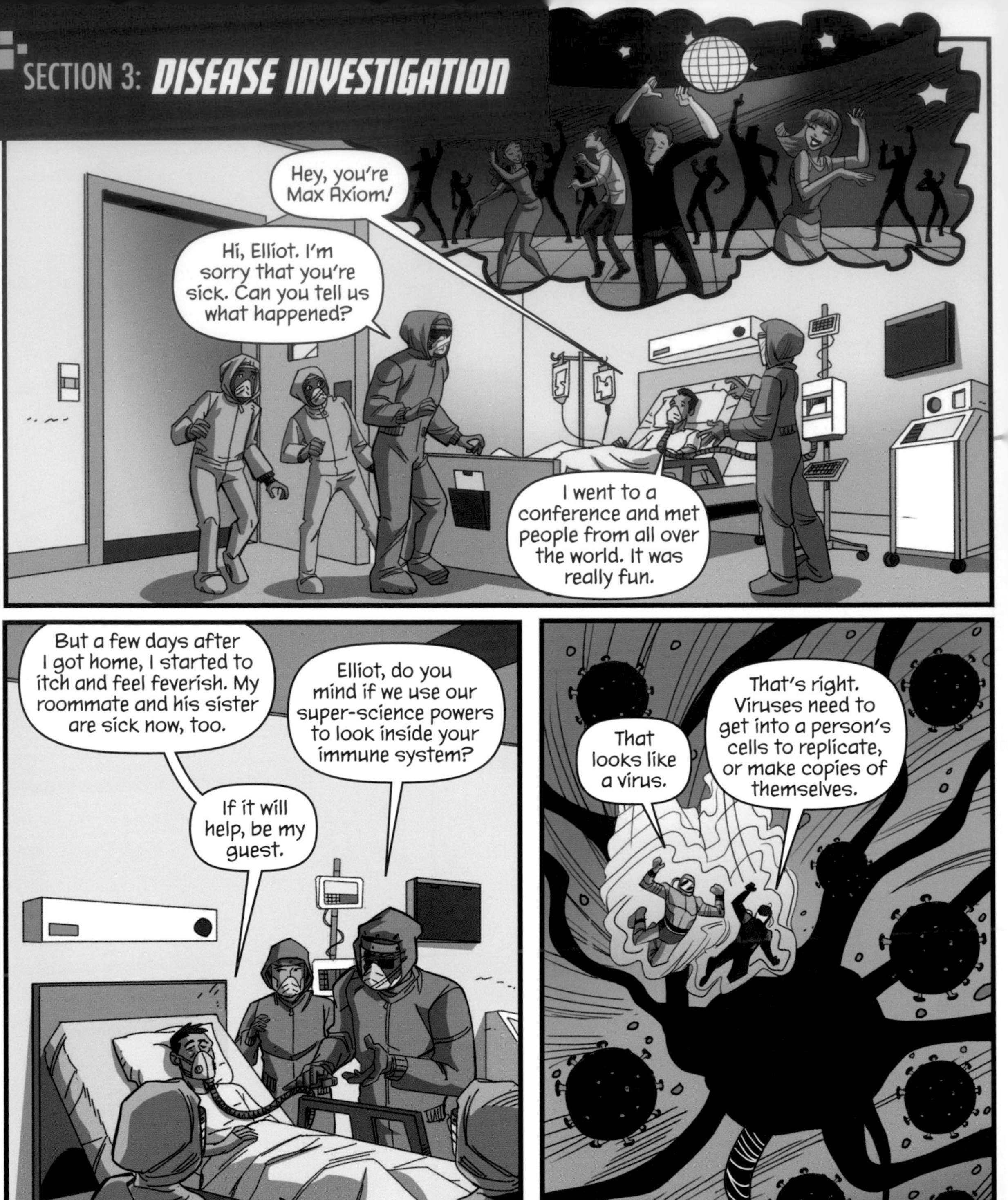
Hi, Elliot. I'm sorry that you're sick. Can you tell us what happened?
Hey, you're Max Axiom!
I went to a conference and met people from all over the world. It was really fun.
But a few days after I got home, I started to itch and feel feverish. My roommate and his sister are sick now, too.
Elliot, do you mind if we use our super-science powers to look inside your immune system?
If it will help, be my guest.
I'll stay here and keep you company.
That looks like a virus.
That's right. Viruses need to get into a person's cells to replicate, or make copies of themselves.

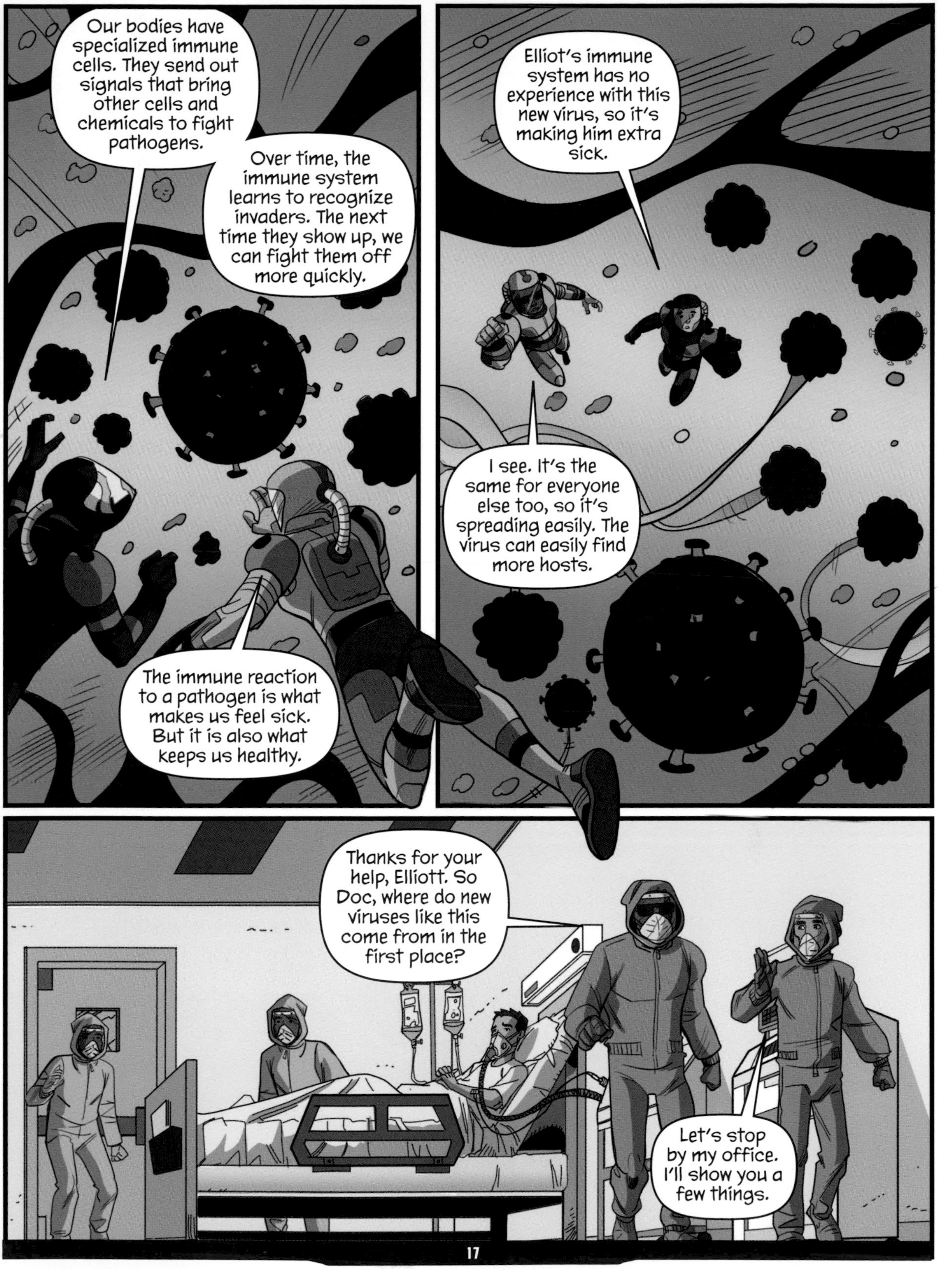

Our bodies have specialized immune cells. They send out signals that bring other cells and chemicals to fight pathogens.
Over time, the immune system learns to recognize invaders. The next time they show up, we can fight them off more quickly.
The immune reaction to a pathogen is what makes us feel sick. But it is also what keeps us healthy.
Elliot's immune system has no experience with this new virus, so it's making him extra sick.
I see. It's the same for everyone else too, so it's spreading easily. The virus can easily find more hosts.
Thanks for your help, Elliott. So Doc, where do new viruses like this come from in the first place?
Let's stop by my office. I'll show you a few things.

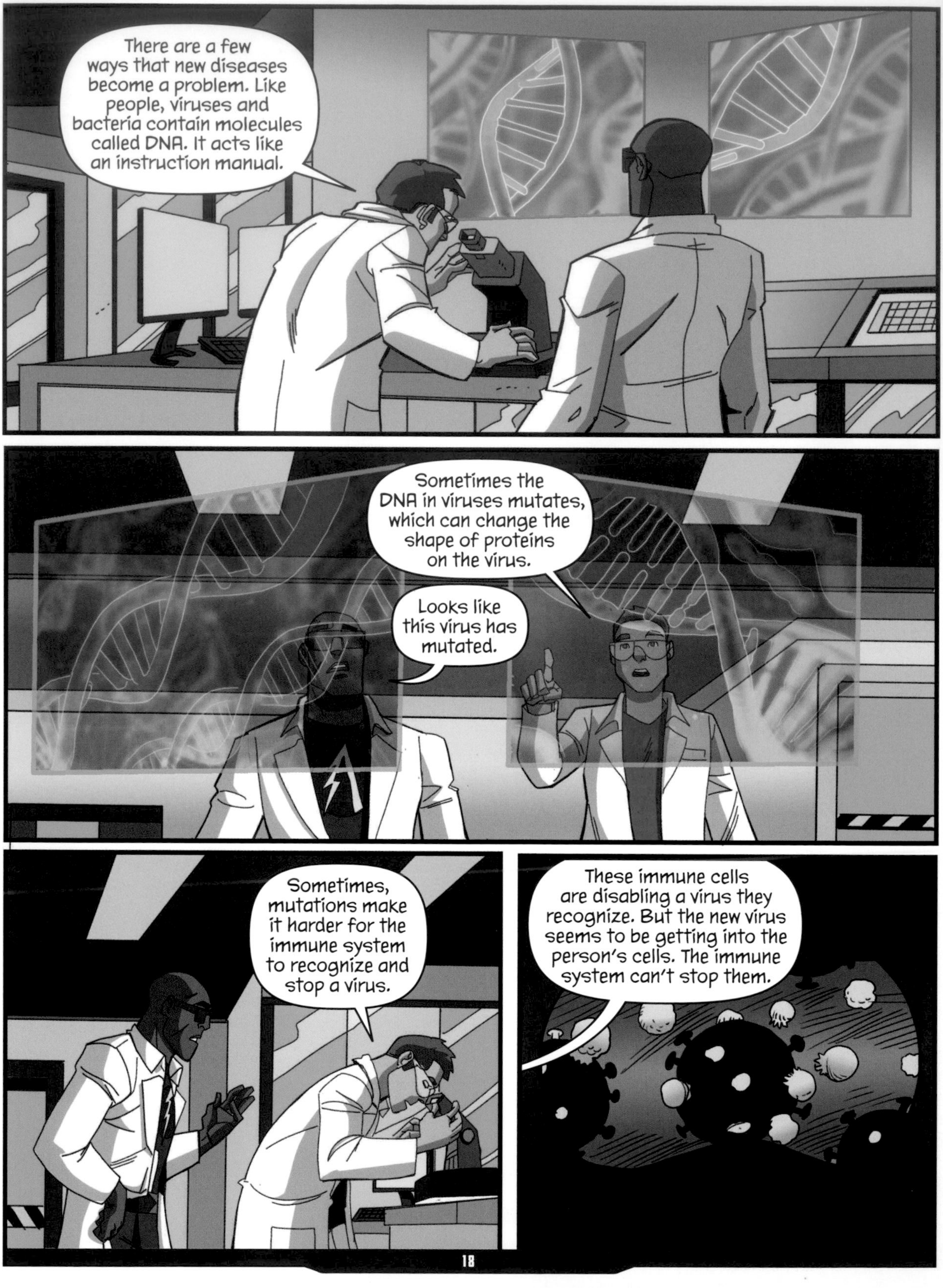
There are a few ways that new diseases become a problem. Like people, viruses and bacteria contain molecules called DNA. It acts like an instruction manual.
Sometimes the DNA in viruses mutates, which can change the shape of proteins on the virus.
Looks like this virus has mutated.
Sometimes, mutations make it harder for the immune system to recognize and stop a virus.
These immune cells are disabling a virus they recognize. But the new virus seems to be getting into the person's cells. The immune system can't stop them.

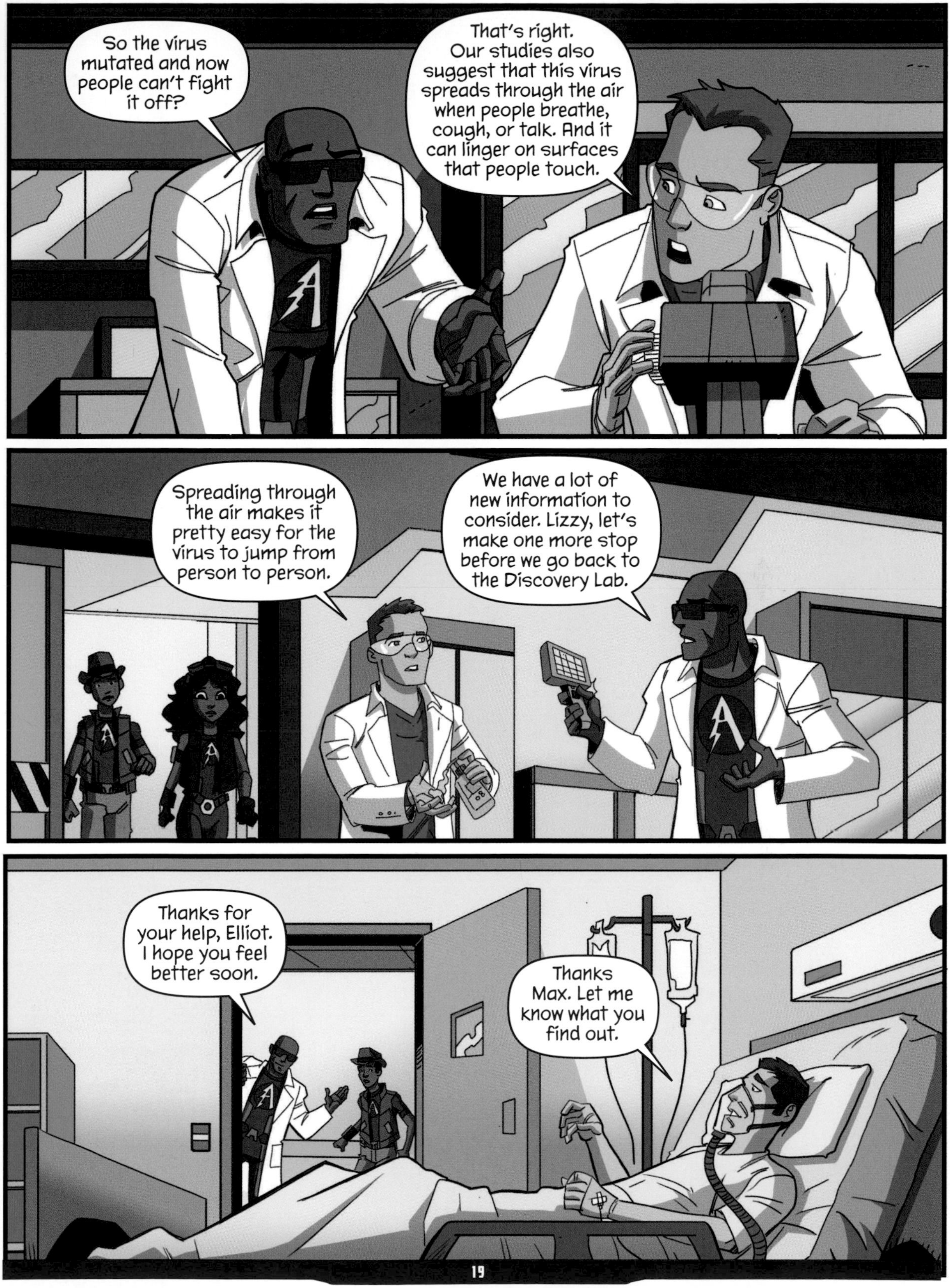
So the virus mutated and now people can't fight it off?
That's right. Our studies also suggest that this virus spreads through the air when people breathe, cough, or talk. And it can linger on surfaces that people touch.
Spreading through the air makes it pretty easy for the virus to jump from person to person.
We have a lot of new information to consider. Lizzy, let's make one more stop before we go back to the Discovery Lab.
Thanks for your help, Elliot. I hope you feel better soon.
Thanks Max. Let me know what you find out.

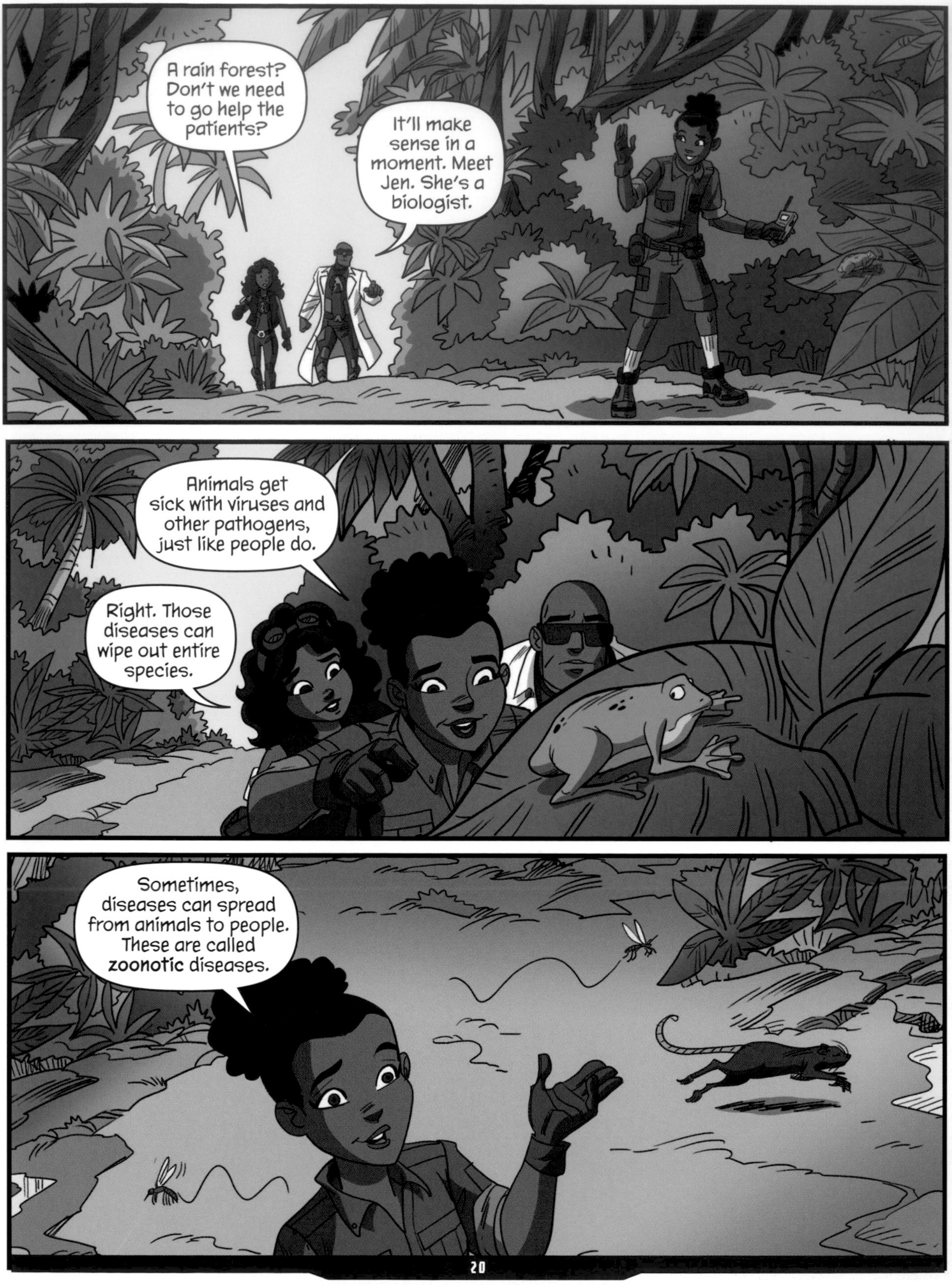
A rain forest? Don't we need to go help the patients?
It'll make sense in a moment. Meet Jen. She's a biologist.
Animals get sick with viruses and other pathogens, just like people do.
Right. Those diseases can wipe out entire species.
Sometimes, diseases can spread from animals to people. These are called **zoonotic** diseases.

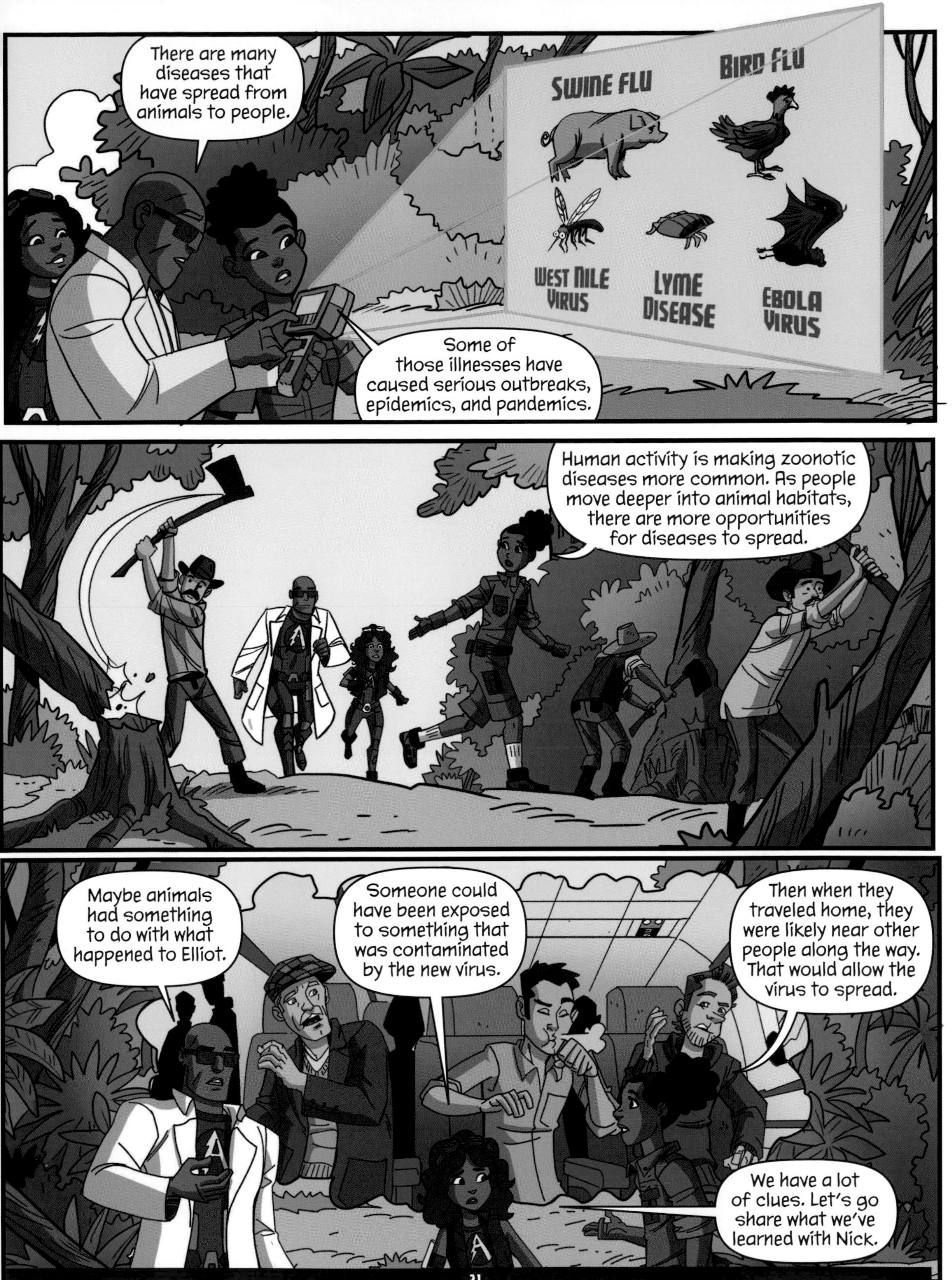
There are many diseases that have spread from animals to people.
SWINE FLU
BIRD FLU
WEST NILE VIRUS
LYME DISEASE
EBOLA VIRUS
Some of those illnesses have caused serious outbreaks, epidemics, and pandemics.
Human activity is making zoonotic diseases more common. As people move deeper into animal habitats, there are more opportunities for diseases to spread.
Maybe animals had something to do with what happened to Elliot.
Someone could have been exposed to something that was contaminated by the new virus.
Then when they traveled home, they were likely near other people along the way. That would allow the virus to spread.
We have a lot of clues. Let's go share what we've learned with Nick.

SECTION 4: FIGHTING BACK

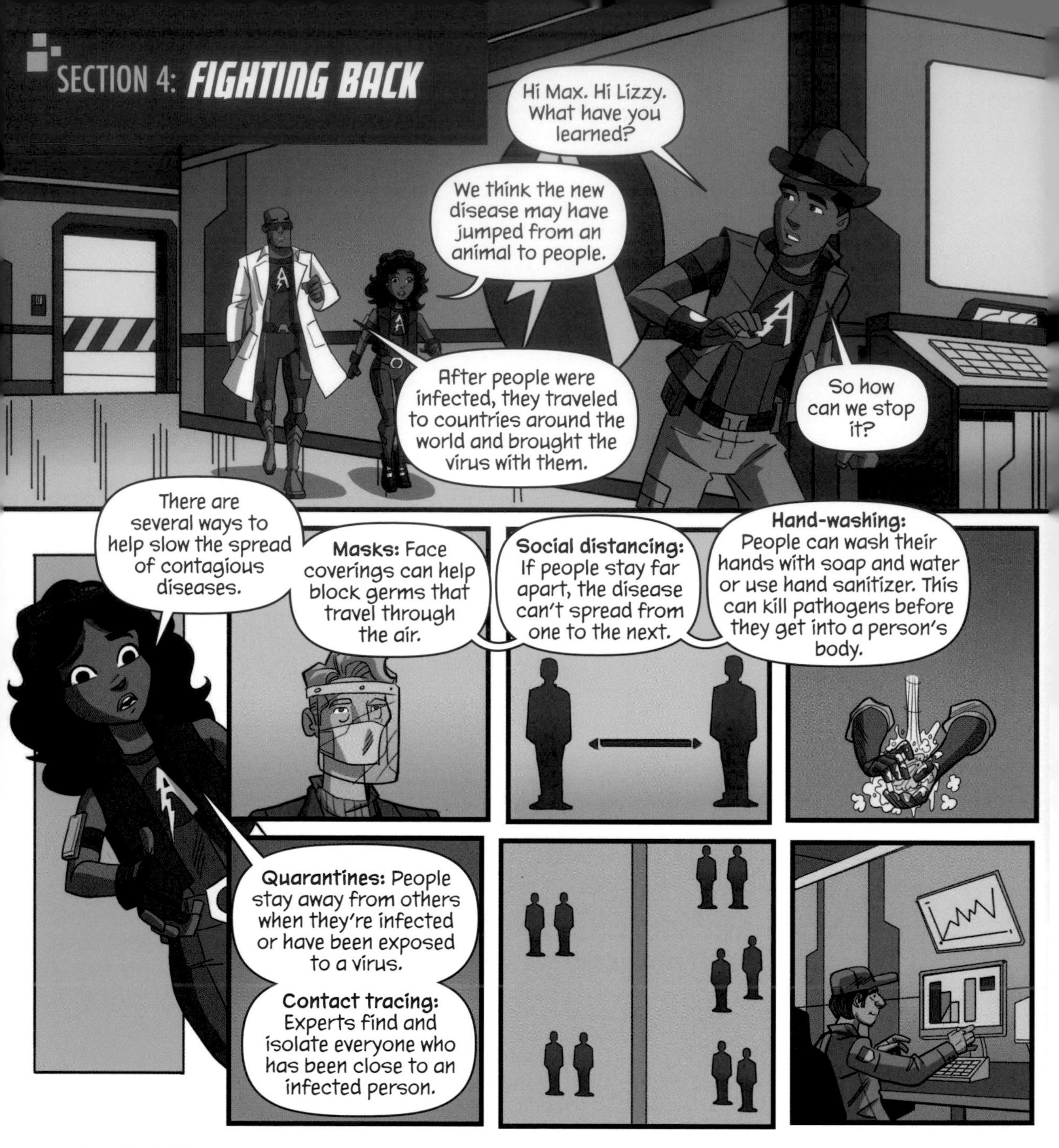

Hi Max. Hi Lizzy. What have you learned?
We think the new disease may have jumped from an animal to people.
After people were infected, they traveled to countries around the world and brought the virus with them.
So how can we stop it?
There are several ways to help slow the spread of contagious diseases.
Masks: Face coverings can help block germs that travel through the air.
Social distancing: If people stay far apart, the disease can't spread from one to the next.
Hand-washing: People can wash their hands with soap and water or use hand sanitizer. This can kill pathogens before they get into a person's body.
Quarantines: People stay away from others when they're infected or have been exposed to a virus.
Contact tracing: Experts find and isolate everyone who has been close to an infected person.

COVID-19

The COVID-19 pandemic was first identified in China in late 2019. The virus rapidly spread all over the world. Countries used many strategies to try to stop the virus from infecting more people, including quarantines, mask orders, and contact tracing.

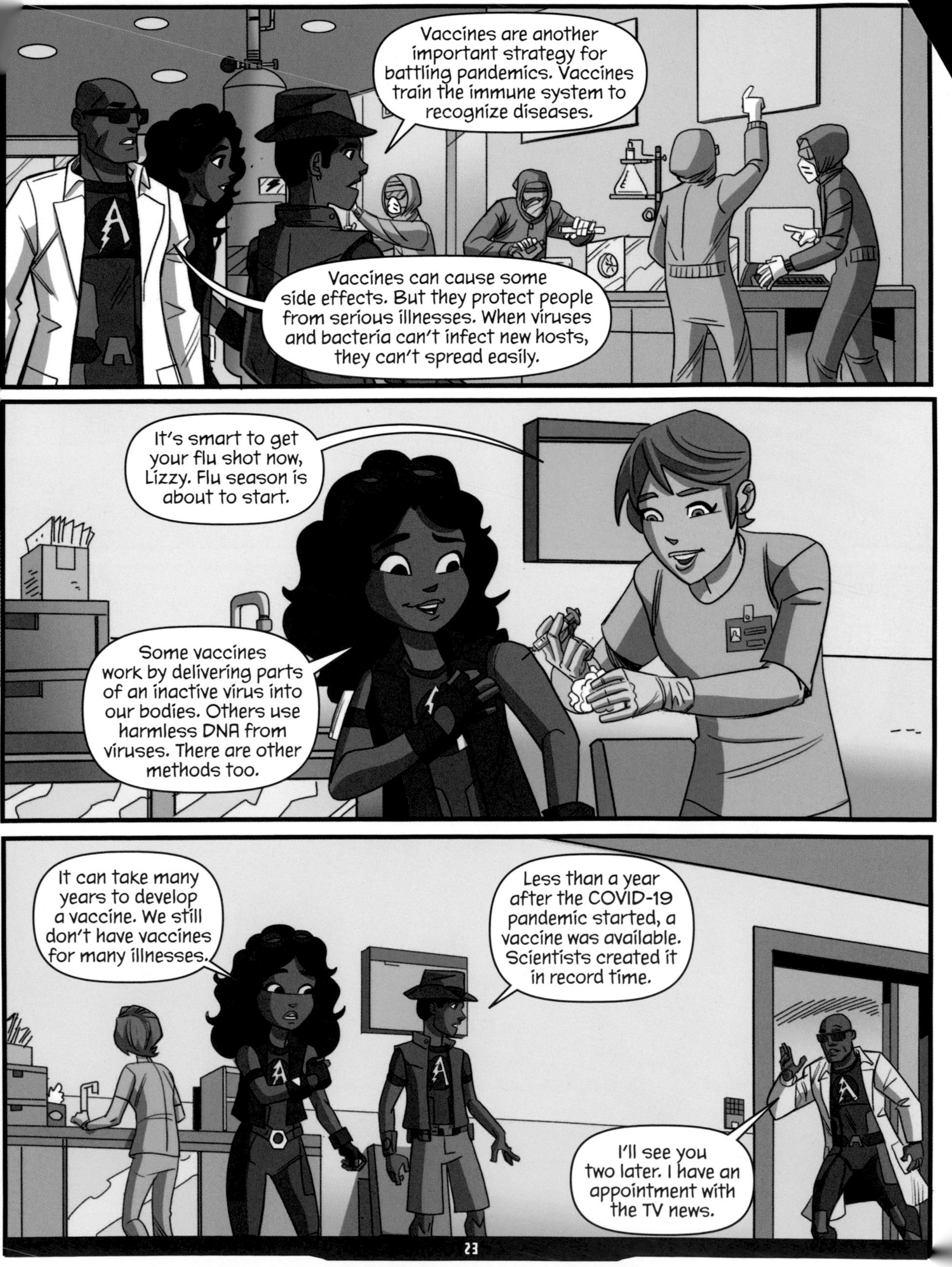
Vaccines are another important strategy for battling pandemics. Vaccines train the immune system to recognize diseases.
Vaccines can cause some side effects. But they protect people from serious illnesses. When viruses and bacteria can't infect new hosts, they can't spread easily.
It's smart to get your flu shot now, Lizzy. Flu season is about to start.
Some vaccines work by delivering parts of an inactive virus into our bodies. Others use harmless DNA from viruses. There are other methods too.
It can take many years to develop a vaccine. We still don't have vaccines for many illnesses.
Less than a year after the COVID-19 pandemic started, a vaccine was available. Scientists created it in record time.
I'll see you two later. I have an appointment with the TV news.

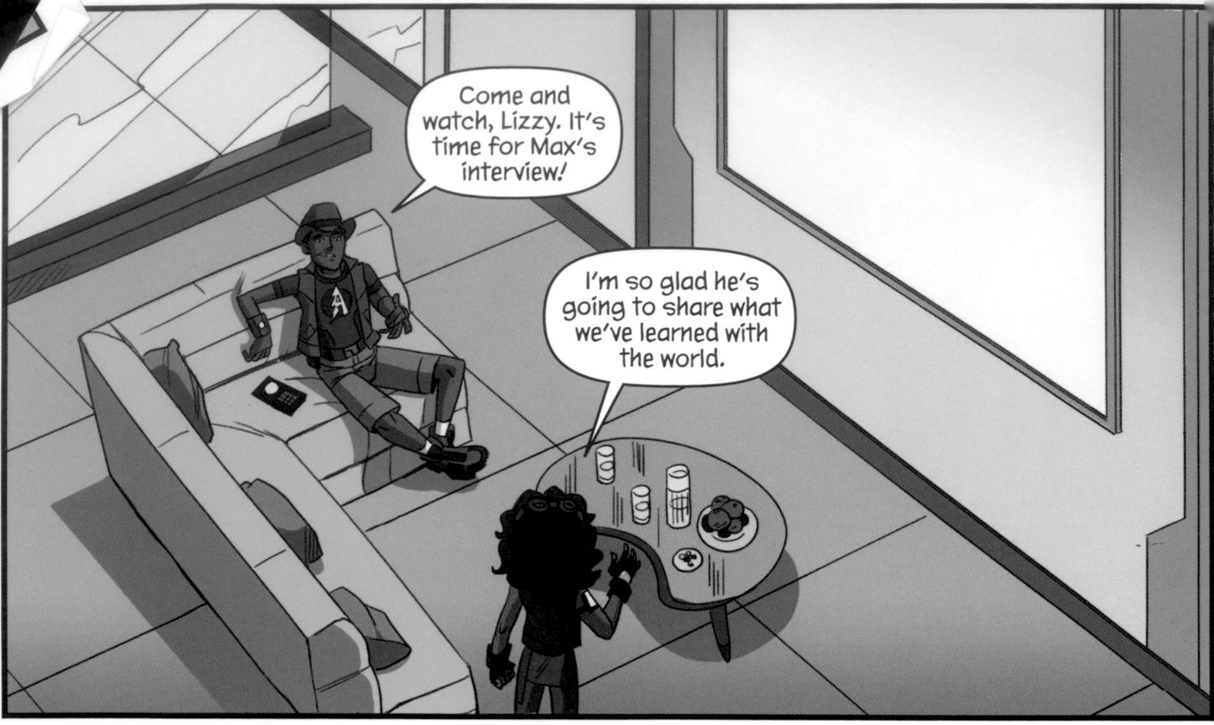
Come and watch, Lizzy. It's time for Max's interview!
I'm so glad he's going to share what we've learned with the world.

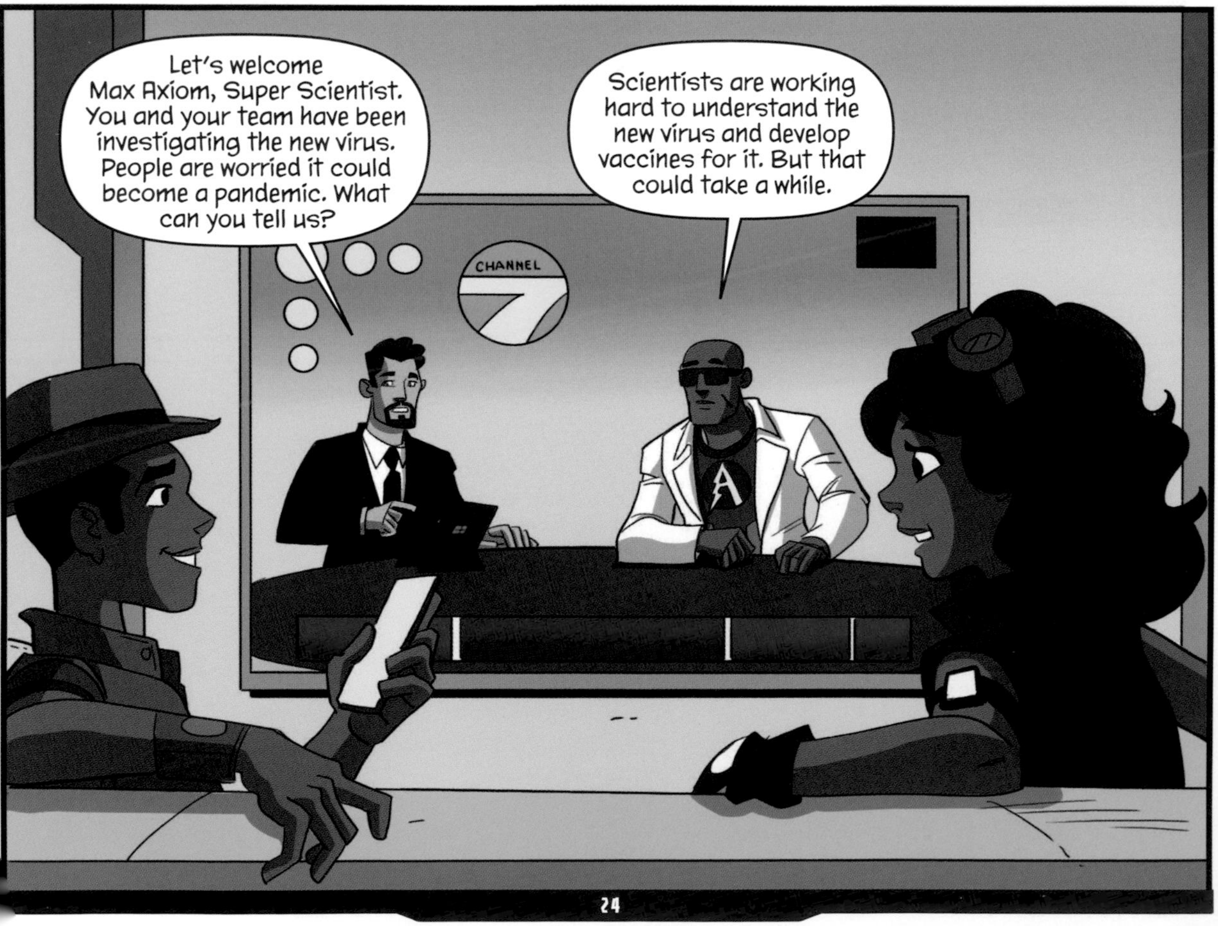
Let's welcome Max Axiom, Super Scientist. You and your team have been investigating the new virus. People are worried it could become a pandemic. What can you tell us?
Scientists are working hard to understand the new virus and develop vaccines for it. But that could take a while.
CHANNEL
7

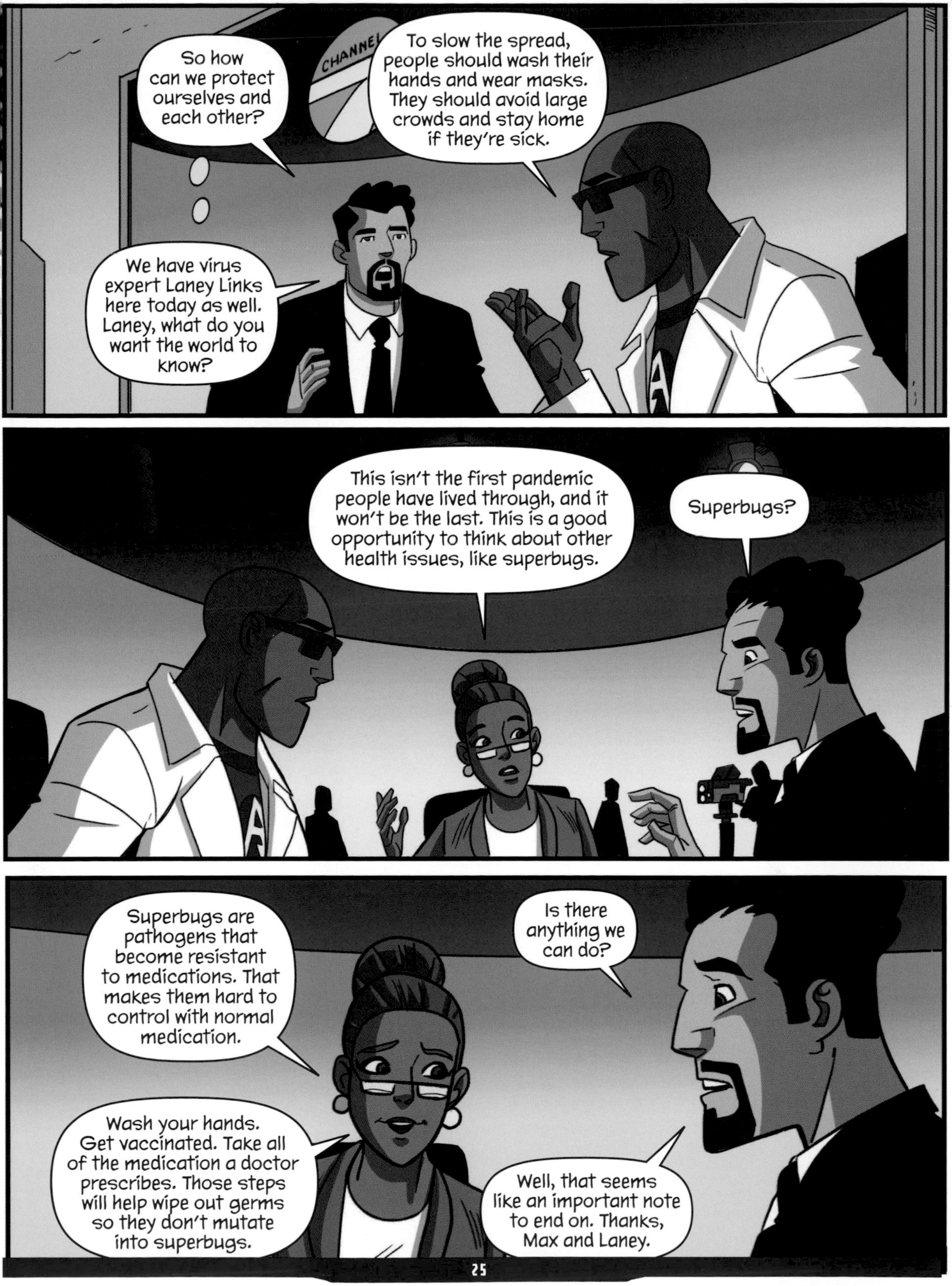

So how can we protect ourselves and each other?
To slow the spread, people should wash their hands and wear masks. They should avoid large crowds and stay home if they're sick.
CHANNEL
We have virus expert Laney Links here today as well. Laney, what do you want the world to know?
This isn't the first pandemic people have lived through, and it won't be the last. This is a good opportunity to think about other health issues, like superbugs.
Superbugs?
Superbugs are pathogens that become resistant to medications. That makes them hard to control with normal medication.
Is there anything we can do?
Wash your hands. Get vaccinated. Take all of the medication a doctor prescribes. Those steps will help wipe out germs so they don't mutate into superbugs.
Well, that seems like an important note to end on. Thanks, Max and Laney.

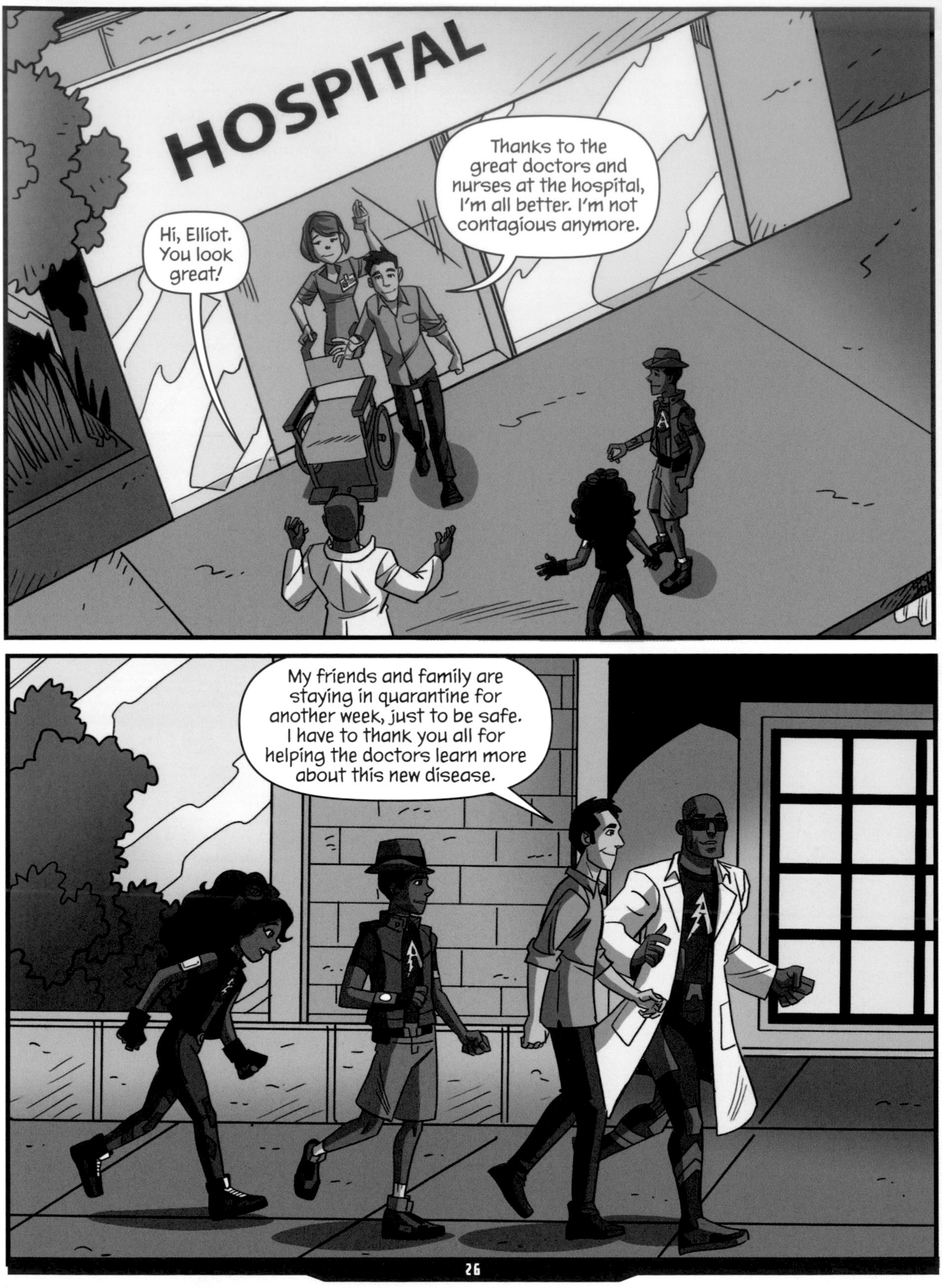
HOSPITAL
Hi, Elliot. You look great!
Thanks to the great doctors and nurses at the hospital, I'm all better. I'm not contagious anymore.
My friends and family are staying in quarantine for another week, just to be safe. I have to thank you all for helping the doctors learn more about this new disease.

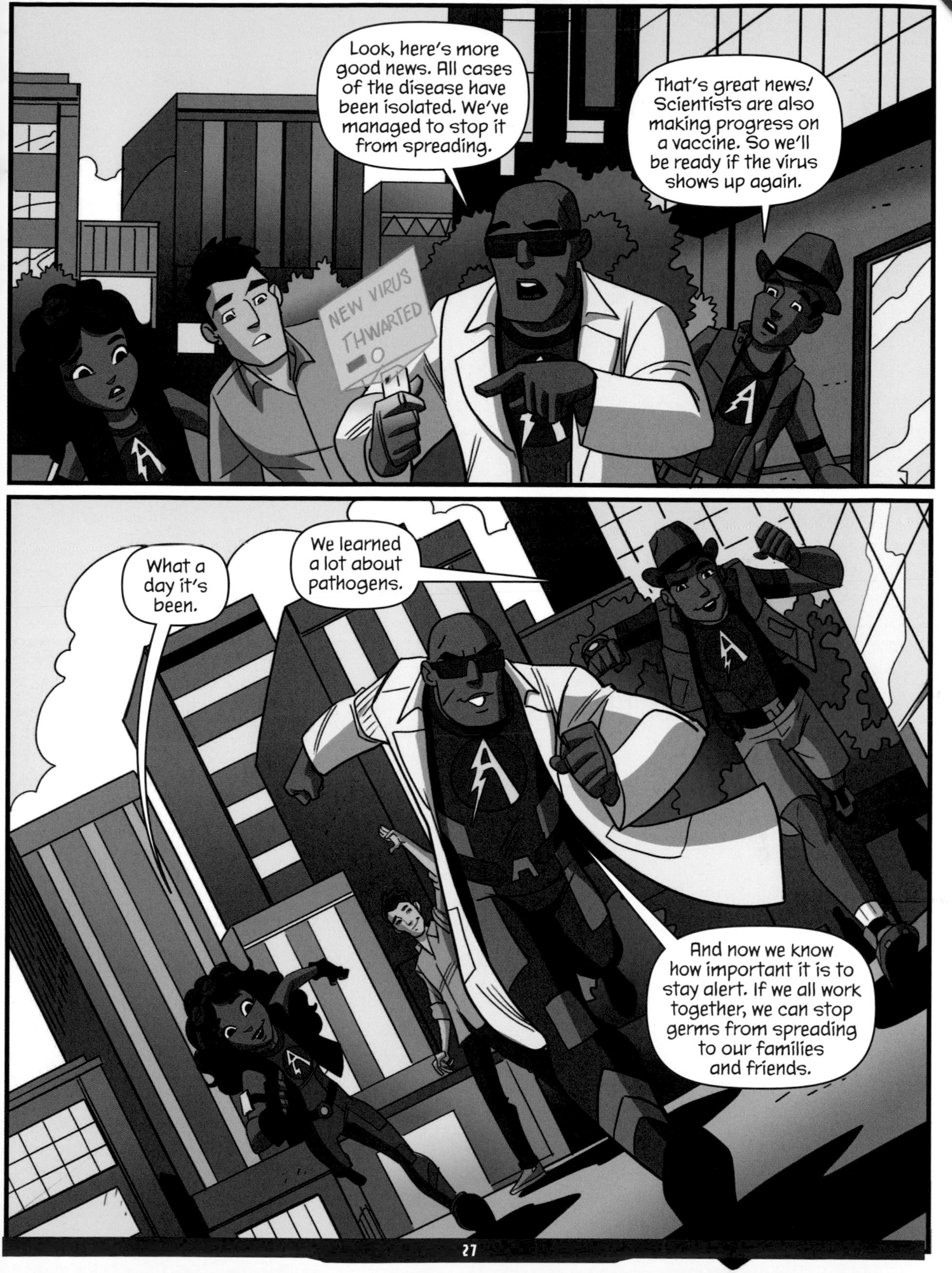
Look, here's more good news. All cases of the disease have been isolated. We've managed to stop it from spreading.
NEW VIRUS THWARTED
That's great news! Scientists are also making progress on a vaccine. So we'll be ready if the virus shows up again.
What a day it's been.
We learned a lot about pathogens.
And now we know how important it is to stay alert. If we all work together, we can stop germs from spreading to our families and friends.

MORE ABOUT PANDEMICS

In 2020, the COVID-19 pandemic began to spread around the world. More than 180 million people got sick from the virus, which causes high fevers, coughing, loss of taste and smell, and other symptoms. By the fall of 2021, more than 4.5 million people had died around the world, including nearly 700,000 in the United States.

The COVID-19 pandemic shut down much of the world. Governments in many countries ordered people to stay home for weeks or months. When people were allowed to travel again, there were rules about wearing masks and staying apart from others.

The COVID-19 shutdowns caused a lot of hardships for people. Businesses closed. Millions of people lost their jobs. Millions of children had to stay home from school. A lot of people felt lonely and depressed. Experts argued about whether closing everything was worse than the virus. But others thought that many more people could have died without the restrictions. There were no easy answers.

The 1918 influenza pandemic was the most severe pandemic before COVID-19. An estimated 500 million people got infected with it. That was a third of all the people living on Earth! More than 50 million died around the world from the 1918 flu, including about 675,000 in the United States.

Scientists made vaccines for COVID-19 in record time. A lot of vaccines take many years to create. But several effective COVID-19 vaccines were ready in less than a year.

There are millions of types of viruses and bacteria in the world. Most don't make us sick. Many live in and on us at all times.

Every year, drug-resistant superbugs infect nearly 3 million people in the United States.

GLOSSARY

antibiotic (an-tee-bye-OT-ik)—a drug that kills bacteria and is used to cure infections and disease

contagious (kuhn-TAY-juhs)—carrying or spreading a disease from person to person

DNA (dee-en-AY)—the material in body cells that carries instructions to make a living thing and keep it working; DNA stands for deoxyribonucleic acid.

host (HOHST)—a living thing or cell that serves as a home or source of food for another living thing, such as a parasite, virus, or bacteria

immunity (ih-MYOO-ni-tee)—being able to resist or fight off disease

mutate (MYOO-tayt)—to change

pathogen (PATH-uh-jen)—a microorganism that causes disease

saliva (suh-LYE-vuh)—the clear liquid in your mouth produced by glands under the tongue and in the jaw

species (SPEE-sheez)—a group of plants or animals that share common characteristics

strain (STRAYN)—a bacteria or virus that causes symptoms similar to another but has unique characteristics

superbug (SOO-per-buhg)—a bacteria that has become resistant to common antibiotic medications

symptom (SIMP-tuhm)—a sign, such as a cough or a fever, that a person has an illness or is infected

vaccine (vak-SEEN)—a medicine that prevents a disease

zoonotic disease (zoh-on-OT-ik di-ZEEZ)—a disease caused by a germ that spreads from animals to people

READ MORE

Farndon, John. *Plague! Epidemics and Scourges Through the Ages.*
Minneapolis: Lerner Publishing Group, Inc., 2017.

Platt, Richard and John Kelly. *The Germ Lab: The Gruesome Story of
Deadly Diseases.* New York: Kingfisher, 2020.

Throp, Clair. *The Horror of the Bubonic Plague.* North Mankato, MN:
Capstone Press, 2018.

INTERNET SITES

Biology for Kids: Epidemics and Pandemics
ducksters.com/science/biology/epidemics_and_pandemics.php

The History of Pandemics
timeforkids.com/g56/history-pandemics/

Outbreaks, Epidemics, and Pandemics
kidsboostimmunity.com/outbreaks-epidemics-and-pandemics

INDEX

ABOUT THE AUTHOR

Emily Sohn is a freelance journalist in Minneapolis who covers mostly health, science, the environment, and adventure for both kids and grown-ups. Her work has appeared in *The New York Times*, *National Geographic*, *Nature*, *The Washington Post*, and many other publications. Assignments have taken Emily to exotic locations around the globe, including Cuba, Fiji, and the Peruvian Amazon.